Unacceptable

Strength is made perfect in weakness.
Philippians 4:13

UNACCEPTABLE

One Black Sheep's Journey to Acceptance

CHAPLAIN (LTC), U.S. ARMY (RETIRED),
LESLIE SIMONSON

Unacceptable

ISBN: 978-1-926718-14-9

Cover Design: Christine Delano
Book Design: Andrew Mackay
Managing Editor: Rick Johnson
Published by

Dedication

This book is being dedicated to, first and for most, my Lord and Savior Jesus Christ who has given me the "peace that passes all understanding" and eternal salvation thru his shed blood on the Cross. He also gave me the power that I needed to witness to the glory and power of our Lord and Savior through the Baptism of the Holy Spirit.

Then to my wife Sharon, who has been my best friend and help mate these many years. Thru it all she has remained faithful as she packed up our household, more times than I care to remember, and together with the children followed me in a journey that many times she , I am sure, knew not where it would end. Sharon and all of our four children, Timothy, Philip, Ruth, and Erik lived the journey, each in their own way and many times had to put up with many not so pleasant experiences that I unfortunately did not know about until much later in life. For this I am truly sorry but thank them all for their faithfulness along the way. And I love you all very much. To that end I dedicate the book to each of you. Thanks a bunch you guys.

Finally, I am dedicating this work to my parents, Lyle and Bernice Simonson, who gave me a chance at life, having to raise four children during two wars, WWII and Korean, with very limited resources, and who yet saw to it that we had food to eat and made sure that we went to church every Sunday, and Sharon's parents, Gordon and Harriet Glover who had it plenty hard raising seven children during the same time, (all of whom are now deceased). Our parents deserved more than they got for being such a major part of our lives and am only sorry that they could not have been able to get the full story of what was going on in our lives those years and many times had only to go by faith and trust in us when they were only able to get part of the facts. For this I am truly grateful and only wish they could have been here to share this time with us, and get the full story.

Acknowledgments

When Ralph Kessler, a good friend and fellow pastor encouraged and even had the audacity to suggest that I write up this story and even gave the title for this work *UNACCEPTABLE,* that he informed me the Lord had given him to tell me. My reaction at the time was humor him but forget him. Forget him I did for several years but never was quite able to get this admonition of Ralph's out of my mind.

And so it was that I began, first writing in long hand on legal pads as I ministered to troops along the way around the world. Thinking about Life and ministry with the work that the Lord had given me... And so to Ralph I am grateful.

I must not forget Dr. Gene Neill, a very close friend and fellow pastor and best selling author of *I'm Gonna Bury You,* for reading my manuscript and give very helpful suggestions on how to write successfully. And writing a foreword for my book.

Then finally want to thank Chaplain Jim Ammerman, a fellow Army chaplain who later came my endorser for the chaplaincy with the Chaplaincy Full Gospel Churches, who mentored me along the way on my journey and was also very kind to read the manuscript for final suggestions.

Special thanks go to Sharon again for all of her patience and understanding together with the many helpful suggestions and support when I wanted to quit the job, she always encouraged me to continue in the typing and retyping of the manuscript. She had a great deal to do with the ultimate completions of the project. And I must not forget to thank our son Erik , who retyped the final manuscript to be ready for the publisher.

A special word of thanks to our publisher Gus Henne for all his support and encouragement along the way in this journey. His unique sense of humor and pleasant ways and encouragement have meant a lot to me in the whole process, making it very easy indeed.

Last but not least, by any means Sharon and I are grateful to our Lord and Savior, Jesus Christ for His bringing us together and giving us this challenge in the journey of hope, joy, and yes even pain and suffering and sorrow with the final promise of eternal life. For truly without Him, none of this would have been possible.

Contents

Foreword

My dear brother Les–

I have finally completed your delightful manuscript, and very honestly enjoyed it immensely!

It's a real story of how a real God can work in the life of a real man. A charming account of how Christianity—and Christians—work.

If I were a Christian looking for a book to read—I would choose yours!

But I don't believe the publisher will.

Christians—particularly of the "Charismatic" variety are looking for thrills, roaring excitement.

People walking on water and being raised from the dead, and all that jazz.

That's not the way it should be, but that's the way it is.

The book of Ruth would never sell in today's Christian market.

I would go ahead and give some publishers a shot at it if I were you,. But if they send you a pink slip don't think for a moment that it's your fault.

It's their fault.

Love always,
Gene and Dorothy Neill

Dr. Gene Neill is the author of the book *I'm Gonna Bury You,* a best seller with over 590,000 books in print.

Preface

*Jesus Christ was the full reve-*lation of what God intended man to be. The very fullness of the Godhead was in him. Christ has provided man everything that is needed for life and godliness. By his grace, He made it possible for one to experience Christ within. Christ within is the only hope of worth, dignity and adequacy.

Insightful people have come to abdication of personal sovereignty; have ceased from their struggles to save themselves. They have permitted Christ to rule and reign in their lives. What a significant discovery to find peace as they cease their works. The secret is simply letting Christ in them, live the life, permitting Him full expression.

The church, the Body of Christ, should likewise be the expression of everything God intended corporate life to be. The community of believers should demonstrate affinities, acceptance, love, and relationships as God intended them to be. It should be a caring, healing, helping family of God. It should be a body with each member functioning in divine order, each member submitting to the coordinating impulses of the Holy Spirit.

But alas, the body instead is fragmented, uncoordinated, and foundering. It's functioning is frustrated by its lack of real commitment to Christ and placement of personal gain and tradition over loyalty to

Christ. The placement of institutional values above personal faith in Jesus Christ has been the cause of much suffering in the body.

This work is a muffled voice in the wilderness of humanly devised institutional values and priorities that have been unconsciously absorbed by the institutional church. Much like a society, as it were, that has unwittingly been consuming health destroying junk food and contaminated food, so the institutional church, unaware, has found itself conforming to the world's values.

This study is an urgent call to all who may read to return again to the design of a revival of personal relational faith in Jesus Christ that stands out as above and beyond institutional beliefs, and convictions, no matter how sincere. Through a personal case study, this work, is calling the church, the Body of Christ, to be the expression of everything God intended corporate life to be. Mainly, a community of believers demonstrating affinities of acceptance, love and relationships as God intended them, in a caring, helping and healing environment.

I wish to acknowledge the significant assistance of my dear wife, Sharon. Her patience and understanding together with helpful suggestions during the long hours of typing and retyping have virtually made this book possible.

I wish to express appreciation to Bobbi Stricker for her typing of the final draft. No small task in itself.

Finally, I appreciate California Graduate School for the opportunity of exposure to men and women of stature who have inspired and stimulated. Special thanks is due Dr. June McBernie who encouraged the pursuit of this subject, and who consented to become involved with me as advisor.

Introduction

Where does one began when trying to acknowledge those who have touched a life and made significant impact on it. My story is not in any way unique in that regard. It is true that due to the fact that having been thru what I have experienced many lives have been touched , well at the same time I have had the experience of visiting and working in and thru a variety of different churches.. The most significant being the Lutheran Church. I will be forever grateful to my parents who took me to church where I would hear the Word of God and be baptized and confirmed . I will be trying to show the significant difference between organized religion and personal faith in Jesus Christ. There will be those who disagree, and I understand that. But, all I can do is tell what happened to me. Not to offend anyone or put their faith down... The task may be a bit difficult, but not impossible... As a result of this personal struggle to find peace with God and then to serve Him faithfully I will try to show how He would allow me to experience a number of different denominations. Some of which I had unfortunately been conditioned against and had been led to believe were not right or theologically correct.

Part of the burden of this book will be to try to explain, to those interested, how I came to a personal faith in Jesus Christ as my Savior and then also to prayerfully experience of the baptism with the Holy Spirit, the benefits to be gained from, and the power that comes along with it as outlined in (Acts 1:8; "But you will receive power when the Holy Spirit comes upon you and you will be my witnesses....."). It was that experience that changed everything for me. Thru this experience many were in the process, at times, offended by my seemingly insensitive and bold decisions. For those who were and are offended , I am truly sorry and wish them no ill will whatsoever.

My story is not in anyway unique in that I have lived those experiences that I learned in the process of growing up, as the saying goes "We learn what we Live!" My intent is not in any way to be critical of any person or institution but rather to try to share, with anyone interested, my journey to faith as honestly as possible. In doing so, it has been my hope that others will experience some of same things that I have experienced in Christian growth. Personal faith in Jesus Christ and the power of His Holy Spirit that has made the journey worth it. And in the final analysis, when all is said and done, this book is not really about me at all. I would like to suggest it is more about the experiences, habits. Successes and failures that we all have in our lives that lead us to becoming winners or losers in life. Feeling acceptable or unacceptable is a major part of that. I have a saying that has stuck with me thru the years that sums this up. "We learn more from Failure than we do from Success."

And finally a quote from Oral Roberts that I remember from one of his sermons: "The most dangerous time in our lives is when we DON'T HAVE to have faith."

I close with a quote from C. S. Lewis, writer of *Mere Christianity* and many other great works, That I recently came across in a book on his life written by his stepson Douglas Gresham. He was quoting Mr Lewis when he was giving some advice on writing: Jack told me, "First be sure that you know exactly what you want to say. Then be sure you have said exactly that." I have tried very hard to follow his advice myself. Only you, the reader, will be able to give the grade on how well I have accomplished this challenge.

My hope and prayer is that I will be able to show how an ordinary person can live a extraordinary life with the power of the Holy Spirit at work in their lives, and if we allow Him to, can make us far more than we could ever be by ourselves.

Professional Killers!

It was a hot July day in 1956, with the temperature at 115 degrees in the shade. I was standing on the parade field at Fort Carson, Colorado. I'd just finished sixteen grueling weeks of infantry training.

"It's hot as hell out here!", one soldier yelled, as another dropped from the heat and hit the dirt. Men had been dropping all over the place for the last hour, as we waited for the parade to start.

The 8th Infantry Division had completed training and would leave soon for Germany.

"How much longer do you think it'll be before this thing gets started?" I asked the guy next to me. "I don't know, but if we don't get outta here soon, I'll be dropping over!" he said.

We continued to talk quietly, as we stood at parade rest, a couple of privates in a back row in that mass of humanity, trying to figure out why we were there.

My thoughts turned to home, as they had so often the past weeks. I wondered how I ever got into this mess in the first place and would have given anything to be out of there and back home for good.

"Maybe it's just a bad dream and I'll soon wake up and find myself home where I belong!" I thought. "Maybe the heats getting to me too!"

"Medic over here in Bravo Company, quick!" someone cried. I knew if something didn't happen soon I'd be a goner. I couldn't take much more.

Then, it happened. A loud booming voice, seemingly from out of nowhere announced,"Gentlemen! You are now Professional Killers! Killers! Killers...the voice echoed over the P.A. system and then drifted away.

And my hair literally stood up on the back of my neck as the sensation like a current of electricity went through me. It went all the way to my boots. Boy, was I scared. "Had I heard right? Did this guy just call me a professional killer?"

Perhaps he's talking to the wrong group, after all, he called us gentleman and I sure hadn't been called anything close to that the past sixteen weeks. I was filled with fear as it registered with me that this was real, I wasn't dreaming, nor was I in the wrong place. The commanding general had arrived and those were the opening words of his speech to his division, of which I was a part.

At once, my mind raced back to when I'd entered the army. I thought of the first night at Fort Leonard Wood, Missouri. How I'd stood in the long column of trainees at 3 o'clock in the morning. Big black Sergeant Parks, the drill instructor, was shouting out names as loud as he could, " Jones, Johnson...Morris, Nevins, Paulie, Roberts..." I knew he was getting closer to me as they reported to him when they were called.

Earlier he'd asked for volunteers to drive truck and when they responded, he laughed good and loud and then sent them up to shovel coal into wheelbarrows for the coal furnaces.

He continued..."Schultz, Schneider, ..." All the time getting closer. Finally I heard, "Simon!" That was close, but not me! Now he called, "Simmons on!" That wasn't me. I'm Simonson. Then he called again, when no one answered, "Simmons on! Are you here!" he yelled. After the third call, I guessed I'd better answer, so I did. "You dumb Son of a Bitch, get up here on the double! What's the matter with you, got a hearing problem?" he screamed.

Lesson learned. Answer to anything close to Simonson, even if they never pronounced it like that back in Mt. Morris. I had a lot of things to learn and didn't have much time in which to do it.

And now, on the parade field, all I could think of was what the general had just said. Professional Killers! I had an argument going on within me. I was no killer! Killing was wrong; I learned that in Sunday school and in church, back home. The general had to be wrong!

Yes, everything within me rejected what he had said. But all at once, it hit me! All the training, what was it for? Why just a few weeks earlier, on the bayonet course, the instructor had yelled, "Come on you stumble bums, let's hear some noise! If you don't start screaming, we'll stay here all night! I wanton hear it now…YAH, YAH, YAH, KILL, KILL, KILL!"

And there it was, Killers! That is what we were trained to be. No matter that I'd always hated violence and fights, we were now trained to do a job, and I didn't want to admit it.

"I don't belong here!" I thought. But knew there was no way out. I'd learned that earlier, and now this!

I thought about the first Sunday on the range, firing the M-1 rifle. "Ready on the right! Ready on the left! Ready on the firing line…Commence Firing!" the range officer yelled out. The rifles cracked and spit out at targets 300 yards down the range.

"Cease Firing! Cease Firing! Cease firing, on the firing line! Clear on the left? Clear on the right… Clear on the firing line! The firing line is clear!" he yelled again.

Then I saw two trucks bounding across the horizon, headed in our direction. "Attention! Attention on the firing line! We have two trucks coming to take those of you who want to got to church!" he blared. "We have one truck for the Protestants and one truck for the Catholics! Report to the tower now, if you want to go!"

My mind began to work, "What about the Lutherans? Don't we count? Where's our truck? I ***know*** I'm not Catholic…and that Protestant stuff…I don't like the sound of that…I'm Lutheran. I always have been, anyway, and always would be."

I didn't go to church that day! One of the few times that I'd miss, but I had no choice under the circumstances.

This was just the beginning of a real challenge to my faith, something that had never happened before. I know that I needed the Lord, but it seemed like the further away from home I got, the less of him I had, and the more I knew that I needed him.

Meanwhile, back on the parade field, the general continued to talk. Men were still dropping from the heat. I wondered if he saw them and if he even cared. I guessed not, since we were all a bunch of professional killers anyway, what difference would a little heat make?

"If I am a killer, that can only mean one thing. I might be killed, myself!" I thought, as the general was bringing his remarks to a close.

I couldn't deny it any longer; I had to admit it, that's exactly what I am. It was like a moment of truth and I knew I wasn't ready to die.

I now knew I was a "Professional Killer", which is not what I'd had in mind when I volunteered. But, I just knew it.

As I began packing my duffel bag in preparation to depart for Germany, the ringing of the General's words were louder and louder in my mind. "GENTLEMEN, YOU ARE NOW PROFESSIONAL KILLERS!" I couldn't shake 'em, no matter how I tried.

That wasn't the worst of it. I knew that if I was a killer, it could mean only one thing. I might get killed.

The two weeks of leave that I had at home would only make matters worse. As I headed for the airport, I wondered how I'd ever gotten into this mess. "Why did I ever join in the first place?" I left Fort Carson, for the long trip home. My mind flashed back over and over the array of failures, frustrations and fantasies that had brought me here.

All of the failures growing up in Mt. Morris, trying to be accepted, but always causing shame and embarrassment because of my deviation from the accepted standards.

I had many frustrations trying to deal with these strong feelings of insecurity and unacceptability. Frustrations, even then, that caused me untold misery; the fantasy of someday becoming a Five-Star General myself.

My world of reality was coming down upon me. Like an avalanche from atop a steep mountain, sliding and falling suddenly down upon me, I just knew I was going to be buried alive.

Bah, Bah, Black Sheep! Have You Any Wool?

The first thing I thought about on the long trip back home was old grandpa Simonson. He died before I was born. I remembered how grandma had talked about him all the time. She lived with us in Mt. Morris the last years of her life. She was a tough old woman, eighty-six, when she died. I was in the sixth grade at the time.

Grandpa Simonson married grandma Inga in 1885. They lived in Mt. Morris all their lives and had nine children. Dad was one of the youngest to come along.

Grandpa had taken ill with an incurable disease. He worked hard to care for his family. I remember how grandma would tell me how much he loved Jesus, before he died. "he asked all the friends and relatives to come and see him a few days before he passed away and warned them to seek God while there was still time enough." She said often, with tears in her eyes. "He loved Jesus and just before he died he said, 'Now I lay me down and sleep, sweet, in Jesus' arms!'"

I thought again, about death. It wasn't something we talked about at home. When it happened, we just lived through it. Sure it was real, I knew that! I remembered how it was when, as a very small boy, the war broke out and it looked like Dad would have to go. Although it happened a long time ago, now it somehow seemed so close.

Sure, I'd be home, back with my family for a few days, before leaving for Germany. I couldn't stop thinking about death. Not after what the General had said regarding my new profession. His words kept ringing in my mind, "Gentleman, You are now professional killers…"

I thought about that day back in 1941. Boyd, my big brother and I were playing alone in our woodshed playhouse, and I remembered it like it was yesterday.

"C'mon Boyd! Gimmie my truck back or I'm gonna tell mom!" I yelled, "it's mine and I didn't say you could use it!" To which Boyd said, "Shut up or I'll hit you!" That scared me because he'd hit me a lot of times in the past and I didn't want to get it today. "I'll let you have your truck if you give me your tractor!" Boyd added, as we argued in the sand box in our woodshed.

Mother called loudly from the kitchen. "Come in here boys, at once!" the tone of her voice sounded urgent. Usually we never came on the first call, but waited until she had called several times. Somehow, this day seemed different and the call meant that we should respond at once. "Come in here at once," Mother called again.

We both ran into the house to see what was up. I can recall the day and the incident clearly, even though I was just a little past four years of age. Mother was crying! I had not seen her do much crying, something bad must have happened. "War has just been started boys! Daddy may have to be going to the war," she sobbed. We just stood there in the kitchen not really knowing what it was all about.

It was the seventh day of December 1941, the historic day of the bombing of Pearl Harbor by the Japanese. I was only four years old and should have been too young to remember such an event.

Such was not the case, however, since it was such a traumatic event in our family and the impact so heavy and lasting. In the days to follow, we heard a lot about the war, listening to the developments on our radio, the sole link of communication with the outside world.

Life would go on! Mother said many times during the following year, "Daddy may have to go to the war and we will be all alone." That seemed so unreal and my little four-year-old mind could not seem to get a hold of what it meant. I did know that I did not want Mom to be unhappy, which she seemed to be. I sure did not want Dad to leave us and go off to war, even though I had absolutely no idea what war meant.

Archie Bunker talked about World War II a lot on his famous show, and I can relate to a lot of it even if in a rather humorous way. Humor has a way of helping us deal with some of the tragic moments in life. The declaration of the war and the years that followed were nothing less than tragic for us in our little family.

The folks delayed marriage for several years mainly due to the Great Depression on the 1930's. Finally, in 1935, with nothing but a very small family farm and a few milk cows, they were married.

By the time I came along, in 1937, this farm barely provided enough to live on. Charging groceries at the local country store was a common monthly occurrence. I was given the job many times of picking them up. I never remember that we went without food. There was always something on the table to eat and clothes on our backs.

We never had much in the way of luxuries in those early days, but we did have the security and stability of a family. Pearl Harbor did, however, change that for a while.

The first family car that I remember as a lad was the old 1934 Ford two-door sedan. It seemed to me like we drove that car forever. It was at least three years old by the time I was born. Whenever it quit running, Dad would put in another fuel pump. If that didn't do it, he tried a rebuilt carburetor, which was sure to make it good for another year.

Things were different then, in more ways than one. Trips away from home were rare and never over fifty miles. Since the war was on, gas rationing was a way of life and everyone was caught up in the spirit of sacrifice and helping the cause.

The longest trip I recall during the first ten years would be the annual family Christmas get-together that would take us to a different Aunt or Uncle's house each year.

One such trip stands out in my memory. Mother was taking us kids to visit her sister in Winneconne, Wisconsin, about thirty-five miles away.

Our cousin was driving her car, which I believe was a 1939 Ford. It was quite new and had four doors. Ours had only two doors and we were always thrown in the back seat. This trip was no exception as we sped down the highway. The excitement was high. "What should we do when we get there?" Boyd asked. "Let's go down by the river and watch the boats go by!" I suggested, as we chatted and played in the rear seat.

Mother and Inez, our cousin, were talking in the front seat, and moving pretty fast along the highway. "We're really moving, aren't we?" I recall suggesting to Boyd. "Yeah, this is a lot faster than Dad ever goes," he added. We seemed to be having a merry old time with our two little sisters all in the back. It made things rather crowded on the long trip.

"Help! Help!" I yelled. "I'm falling out!" It all happened so fast that there was no time to think. Four little kids in the back seat and two adults in the front. Since we were all used to a two-door, being in a four-door car for the first time was what caused it. Plus, the doors on this old Ford opened differently, in the rear, from today's cars, which, as it turned out may have been what saved my life.

Speeding down the highway at about fifty miles per hour, I suddenly found myself airborne outside the car, hanging on to the door for dear life! I was just behind the drivers seat, and thanks to the quick reaction of my cousin, who was driving, without slowing down, she reached back, somehow, and grabbed me, pulling me back into the safety of the rear compartment of the car. "Wow, that was close...too close for comfort!" my cousin sighed as she braked the car and pulled off along the side of the road. That could have very easily been the end of Leslie Simonson. I guess the Lord was riding with me, even back then. It was an unforgettable experience that became a story that would be told over and over throughout the years to come within our family.

Just another indication that whenever there was trouble in the family, you could just about be sure that Leslie was going to be in the middle of it. It seemed like that to me anyway, always coming up on the short end of the stick or in the middle of the trouble. As the years rolled by, it seemed like that quickly emerged as the pattern. Old Leslie did it again. Yes! Those were the days! The Happy Days at that! Happy days are sometimes sad days, but they all go into the making up of life. Growing up is sometimes painful, sometimes joyful, but never dull. This, I suppose, is true whether one grew up in the nineteen-forties or the nineteen-eighties.

The happy days were not always so happy, however, on the days that I chose to talk back, just once too often, to my Mom. Things had been going bad around the house; I'd been having a bad day, which was not uncommon for me.

"I'm not going to do it!" I yelled. "Oh, yes you are Leslie, or you are going into the closet again!" Mother screamed. "Oh no, not in the closet," I thought to myself. I did not want to go back in there. That is where I was sent when things were really bad and Mom didn't know what else to do with me.

The closet in the parlor was dark, with nothing to do but think about the dark and be afraid of what I could not see. I was always doing both. Once I went in, no telling how long it might be before I got out and the lock was on the outside. It was rough and I feared it. The Parlor was only used when somebody died. And that's where the closet was, a real and scary place.

Yes, the closet was a rough place for a little fellow to be. Especially for a fellow who, it seemed, always had to be on the move. At least it served some purpose. It gave me time to think about how bad I was and how nobody liked me. "I must be really bad to have to be put in a place like this," I would think to myself many times. It did little good to holler and beg to be taken out, for that only made it worse and meant staying in the dark even longer.

In a way, I suppose it would be like going to prison, in solitary confinement. There wasn't anything to be happy about in there.

At least when I did finally get released, as bad as it was, I somehow had the feeling that I had now served my time and paid for the crime and could get a chance to start over. It never really quite worked out that way, but at least, once it was over I could go back to living again and search for the happy days.

Webster defines a woodshed as a place for keeping firewood. Well. That is true, it is that, and more. We had one just off the kitchen and it sometimes stored some other things besides firewood.

"Get in there and stay until you learn to behave yourself," Mother would say, locking the door on me. I usually got put in. Boyd and the girls never got put in as much as I did. Escape was virtually impossible. The only possible route would be the small hole, high and near the roof, used for putting wood in the house.

At least the woodshed was not as bad as the closet. It wasn't dark in there.

One particular day I remember clearly. "Hey, Les! Come on over here," I heard Boyd whisper. "Over by the window, we'll help you out." "Oh, boy", I remember thinking to myself. "This'll be great!" Doug Thorsdad, our neighbor, was with Boyd. He said, "Okay, Les! We'll put a rope down through the hole and you tie it around your belt and then we'll pull you out!" "Okay," I said, "but hurry it up before mom hears us or we'll be in big trouble!"

It worked, and soon I was out and free once again as we took off down the road towards the lake and some fishing. It was short lived, however, for Mom soon discovered me missing. That only made it worse, for now I had the closet again. I was a slow learner and I liked my freedom, even as a youngster. It made for some happy and not so happy days.

I was soon to discover that the happy days didn't end when I finally got the chance to go to school. Nor did the woodshed, for that matter.

You had to be six to start school back in 1943, when I finally started first grade. Boyd started a year earlier, and since he was my main playmate, I missed him a lot. Besides that, I thought surely I was big enough to start school. "Come on Zona, let's walk to school and visit today", I said one day. I had to do a little conning to get her to go, she was pretty straight. However, being only three, I managed convincing her and off we went. It's just about a mile and a half walk from Mt. Morris to our country school. "You go up and knock on the door and I'll wait back here", I said. "Knock! Knock!" Zona went. Quite a sight we were going to visit school. It wasn't long and the door opened. "What's going on here anyway?" Mr. Grahams, the teacher asked. "We have come to visit school today, and see our big brother!" Zona said as I stood peeking around the corner of the door. I let her do all of the dirty work, since I somehow knew it wasn't quite the right thing to be doing. And sure enough, we got into big trouble. "You can't be here, you're too young and you'll have to go home! Does your mother know you're here today?", he asked. He was mad and had to let the class out for recess so he could take us across the road to a house that had a phone and call our mother to come and get us at once. They had no phone at the school in those days.

What a way to start a school career, getting kicked out the first day. Things didn't get too much better as the next year I finally was old enough to go.

I would soon learn that the woodshed didn't end when I left home. They even had one at the school and I found out what it was for. Yes, it was a place for keeping firewood, which we burned in the stove at school. It was also used for storing boys who didn't behave.

Yes, the excitement of school soon wore off and I found myself hating it. It became like a prison for me with the only good time being recess and noon. Then I could get free and run and play. The rest of the time got worse and worse as the time went on.

"Okay class, take out a piece of paper and a pencil and get ready for the final spelling test!" Miss Decker said. In fact, she said it every Friday. I dreaded that time more than any other. I couldn't spell worth beans. "Today we have Unit 24 and the first word is Liberty," she added. Twenty-five words later (or fifty, if it was a unit test which came up every sixth week), Miss Decker would say, "Okay now class, turn in your spelling paper and I will grade them. Each word you have spelled incorrectly will have to be copied 100 times each and you'll have to have it finished by Monday morning. Are there any questions?" She concluded. I just knew that I would get no less than twenty-four or twenty-three words wrong. If it were a unit test, it would be forty-five or more. That meant a lot of writing over the weekend. When would I be able to have any fun- go skiing or sledding or anything else!

This is the way it went year after year as it seemed to get worse as time went on. The teachers did everything they could and nothing worked. Leslie was hopeless and would never amount to anything.

I got so bad at arithmetic in the sixth grade that they finally decided that they had to flunk me. Now, I always kind of thought I was stupid, but now there was no doubt about it. I knew it was for sure now.

Yes, spelling tests and the woodshed had a way of taking a lot of happiness out of life for me. I made it tough for a lot of people, too. Most of all my parents, they didn't know what to do with me.

The only real outlet I had was recess and I majored in that. Daydreaming about hitting a home run or scoring a touchdown. I made my mark then and after school.

But there was no doubt about it; Leslie was fast becoming the "Black Sheep" of the family. Whenever there was trouble, I would end up in the middle of it. It's nice to be popular!

That wasn't the way it was. Psychologists tell us we have goals in our misbehavior. Seeking revenge, looking for attention, power, or trying to have our needs met.

Sure I wanted to be accepted, but it seemed like it never happened. Always being rejected and thus feeling unacceptable.

Webster defines "Black Sheep" as a person who causes shame or embarrassment because of his deviation from the accepted standards of the group.

Maybe that's why I started stealing so early in life. Trying to make up for that feeling of rejection and emptiness I was feeling inside. Seemingly, always causing shame and embarrassment, and never quite measuring up to accepted standards.

Three-Time Loser

It was getting dark as the sun slid below the still waters. "It's just about dark enough to get into the barn without being seen", whispered Doug to Tom, Boyd and me. "It shouldn't be any trouble getting in," I added.

What was about to happen was soon to be one of the biggest hauls ever to hit the Retreat barn craft shop, and we were all in position. Yes, we were ready to go in there and get out without missing a single detail. Doug's cousin, Tom, seemed to bring a sense of mystery to the night. He was just in town for the summer and had come from the big, exciting city of Milwaukee. We had planned this event for several weeks, working out every detail. We thought this would be the perfect crime.. It was impossible for us to get caught. As the sun disappeared behind the lifeless water, we moved into action.

"Okay," I whispered, "let's take our positions." Everyone scrambled through the darkness. Boyd took the lookout position by the door and Tom ran to the road so that he could signal Boyd if anyone came down the road. Dough and I were the ones who actually grabbed the goods. We climbed up and went in through an old broken side window. "Man, it's dark in here!" I announced as my body fell to the cement floor. That's one thing we forgot to consider. Lighting! But it was too late now and we were too petrified to turn on any lights. But Doug insisted that he knew exactly where the stuff was and said, "Don't worry about it, it's gonna be O.K." Our eyes soon adjusted to the dark as we felt our way through the shadowy room. We were headed for the crafting section where the "gimp" was located. Gimp was just our word for the plastic string, which came in rolls of a hundred feet. It's primary use was for making bracelets and there was always a large assortment of colors.

"There it is!" Doug cried. "Let's fill the sack and get outta this place!" I quickly agreed and we began shoving rolls upon rolls of the "gimp" into our gunne sack. Just as we were wrapping things up, we hard a voice coming from behind the barn. We both froze in fear, but luckily, it was only Boyd. "Hurry, you guys! Somebody's coming!" We grabbed the goods and headed for the window. We practically climbed the wall as we both climbed through and ran to safety over the bank and down into the marsh on our farm property.

"Boy, am I glad that's over with," I told Doug. We had made a good haul and now it was time to enjoy it.

"Okay you guys, let's not get wild here!" Boyd ordered, "You know we're going to have to hide the stuff until the heat cools down." "I want my share right away," Tom said, " I can take it back to Milwaukee with me and sell it." That's o.k. for him, I thought to myself, but it doesn't help us much. We will have to hide ours and this wasn't something we had thought about before making the haul.

So, we hid the "gimp" in the hay loft of our barn and went on our way. Boys will be boys as we later started to use the stuff up to make some bracelets our mothers began to wonder what it was and where we had gotten it.

"Where is all this stuff coming from that you are making these bracelets with?" my mother asked one day.

About the same time, Doug's mother had asked him the same question, and we were off to the races. What are a couple of honest mothers to do? Here they have three boys with all the evidence and must risk their own reputations and turn us in or cover for us. Hoping that they would do the latter, we waited but to no avail.

It wasn't long before we were loaded into the old 1934 Willis Coupe and headed for the Retreat and Reverend Pape. Before we knew it, we were in the big office. As the story was unfolded, we sat in silence. I guess because our moms had turned us in, Reverend Pape would give us a break. We turned in all but a few rolls of the gimp that we'd hidden in the marsh grass along the creek.

No, crime doesn't pay. It costs! It cost us plenty that year and should have cured us, but it didn't.

We never did forgive Doug's cousin, Tom, and how he had skipped out on us and didn't have to experience what we had went through. Ironically, today, Tom is a detective with the Milwaukee Police Department.

This rather dramatic criminal activity was not the last in my life of crime. I'm not sure why I continued to steal, but I did. Maybe it was the time in which we lived, and the fact that we had very little in the way of material possessions, or perhaps it was because of my feelings of rejection and unacceptability. Whatever it was, I found myself doing it more and more.

I knew it was wrong and I did experience a lot of guilt about it. The guilt came because every time I got caught, the whole family was in a state of shock and felt sure I was on my way to a life of crime as a delinquent, doomed to a life in prison. Worse than that perhaps, was the complete disgrace it was, and would be to the good family name.

But this did little to boost my already faltering self-image and the feeling that was growing within me of complete and utter unacceptability.

I am sure I felt the stealing was not near as bad as getting caught and that was the real crime, getting caught! Of course, along with the stealing always went the lying. I am thankful now for getting caught as much as I did. It was painful at the time but that was the best thing that could have happened to me.

I guess it was about a year after the "gimp" incident that I found myself in another situation. We lived right next to the store, which was the main source of life for us. We did most of our shopping there and the owner of the store, Bob Hartman, was married to a cousin. That made it kind of our store, since he was part of the family.

One day, down at the store, I spotted a new board full of bright, shiny mechanical pencils. Boy did I want one of those for myself. I knew that they cost too much and it would be out of the question to ask mom for one. Besides, I always loved things mechanical. I had to get my hands on it and take it apart to see what made it work.

And like the day, a few years earlier, I spotted the bright watch on Mother's dresser, grabbed it and rant to the barn where I proceeded to pry the back off and check it out. In the process, I panicked and couldn't get it back together. Out of fear, I suppose, I took the whole watch and flung it as far as I could over the high fence, out into the cow yard, behind the barn, which was filled with manure. I thought I had gotten rid of the evidence only to learn later that I would have to face the music. Mother found out. It was another page down for me that I should have learned from, but didn't seem to get the message.

And now, I'm about to pull another job. I was milling around the store looking for the right time. It finally came. Bob wasn't looking now; he was curing up some meat for a customer. So, I grabbed a couple of the shiny pencils and headed for the door. I was home free as I took them to school with me the next day and all was well. That was until that day, back in the store once again, just hanging around, Bob confronted me. "Leslie, why don't you go ahead and bring those pencils that you took back?" I gulped and almost choked on the piece of candy that I was eating at the time. "What pencils are you talking about, I didn't take any!" I said. "Oh, yes you did Leslie, don't try to hide it. I saw you take them; It won't do any good to hide it. You might as well admit to it," Bob continued.

I began to shake and tremble with fear. Yes, fear now of being caught, but more than that- what was going to happen when mother found out. This would be the end. I had hurt her enough already and now this would be more than she could handle.

It was then that a rather unusual thing happened. Very much to my surprise, Bob said, "Why don't you go and get the pencils and bring them back." What was I hearing? I couldn't believe my ears. He continued, "Go ahead and bring them back and we'll keep this thing to ourselves." I wasted no time in agreeing, " I have 'em at school and I will bring 'em back with me tomorrow. Will that be O.K.?" I replied. "That will be just fine, Leslie. Now run along and we'll see you after school tomorrow."

This seemingly small incident had a big impact on me. Here was a man that I had stolen from who was not going to punish me. More than that, he was not going to tell the folks.

I never forgot that incident. As far as I know, he never did tell the folks about it. I know I didn't tell them until years later when I would be able to laugh with them about it.

The incident did not end my career of crime over night. But, it did get me started on the right track away from stealing. I never again took anything from Bob.

"Maybe his religion had something to do with it," I thought. He seemed to be going to church all the time with his family.

It seemed like no matter how hard I tried; I was always bound to come up the loser. I don't know why that was, but I am grateful for it today. If I hadn't been so fortunate to be a three-time loser, it's very possible things could have ended much worse for me.

One further story should serve to establish my credibility as a three-time loser.

It was one Friday night in the fall of 1954. Football season had just ended and things were pretty dead around Mt. Morris. Dean and Dale Glunn, twins and fellow teammates from our championship team had come over. Together with Boyd, we were just horsing around killing time. Now since we weren't into drinking and partying, we were looking for some form of amusement. We soon got it! "Hey! I know what we can do," Dean said. "Old man Hannaman down on the four corners has a great big watermelon patch right along highway 49." He continued, "The melons should be just right now and he claims that no one can get at 'em. I've heard tell he even has armed guards around the patch." Boyd added, " You think we can get 'em without getting caught?" To which Dale said, "I have an idea. Let's take your car (they would know ours), Boyd you drive and let us off on the side road past the patch. Give us about twenty minutes to pick up the melons then pick us up where you let us off. We'll load the melons in and split." "It should work," I added.

That did it. We were set to pull off the Hannaman melon farm. Somehow in the process, we picked up four girls from Red Granite. I'm not sure of the details of how we got them. I guess we figured it would be more fun with some girls around.

"Okay, Boyd let us off here, drive around for twenty minutes before you pick us up," Dale said. We all jumped out of the car and went through the ditch into the patch.

We stumbled and ran through the patch in the dark picking up as many melons as we could all carry and got back over to the road just in time to see Boyd coming back. "Hurry Up!" I yelled. "Get those melons up here on the road, here comes the car!" Just as were finishing the job of loading the melons in the trunk of our 1951 Kaiser, Dean spotted it. "Hey you guys, look down the road, there are some lights coming, we better get outta here, fast!" he yelled. Sure enough, someone had spotted us and was on the run toward us. We all jumped in the car, leaving a few melons behind as they were fast approaching.

Two quick blasts thundered from a shotgun as we sped away to safety.

"Wow, that was close!" we all had laughed as we roared away and found a remote side road to enjoy a feast of cooled watermelons.

It was Saturday morning, I was out on the front porch with my feet propped up just cooling my heels, so to speak. Mom was out by the clothesline hanging out the wash. All at once I looked toward the tavern over the bank to see Leon "Specks" Murty, the Waushara County Sheriff, drive up. I remember thinking to myself, "boy, they must have had some big trouble down there last night." Leon Murty didn't wear glasses, so I guess his nickname "Specks" meant either he couldn't see anything or he that he had a special ability to see all. I'm not really sure which. I always thought he was a good Sheriff...as far as Sheriffs go!

A strange thing happened. "Specks" only had parked at the tavern, but rather came up over the bank and headed for the clothesline and my mother. I guess he was asking her about someone or something. They talked a bit and they soon headed straight to me and the porch. I could see that familiar look in her eyes. This meant, I was in trouble, again. She was not happy, I knew that. As they approached, Mom quickly asked, "Where were you last night?" I gulped, and then, it finally hit me. How could they ever have caught us? We had it all figured out and were sure that we had made a clean get-away. "Nowhere. Why?" I asked wishing that I had gone fishing or to work like Boyd had today, anywhere but being here, now. "Why did I always have to take the rap? After all, it wasn't my idea to get the melons. I just went along for the ride."

Then "Specks" spoke up. "Have a warrant here for your arrest and all seven others who were with you at the four corners and Hanamann's melon patch last night." He continued, "There were four girls in the car too." He went on, "The owner of the patch intends to press charges on all involved and means business. He asked me to notify each of you that he expects to see all of you at his place on this Saturday morning. If everyone doesn't show, he plans to call me and have you all arrested for trespassing and destroying private property."

By this time I was shaking like a leaf and Mom wasn't much better off as she had to hear all of this. Her three-time loser son had done it again and this time it wasn't gimp or mechanical pencils.

"I would advise you to get all involved together and report there on Saturday." And with that, he left and the fun began. Mom was really hurt and had a hard time dealing with this. Our car was involved in a crime and now the family name was ruined for sure.

Needless to say, I wasted no time in getting the word to all that we needed to report on Saturday, or else. After getting a lot of resistance, it was finally agreed on by all that we would be making that trip. It looked like the best bet under the circumstances.

I remember well the visit as we stood before Mr. Hannaman. I realized how wrong it was to do what we had done. He said to us, "Do you realize that by stealing my melons you are taking away from my income to feed my family? I have to live off those melons and that is why I had to have the Sheriff come and get you. I hope you understand that!" he exclaimed. "If you want melons, come down anytime and I would be glad to give you some! Can you see my point?" he added. We said nothing.

There was nothing to say, really. We were in the wrong and what had begun as excitement a few days earlier had turned into something more serious now.

Then he continued, much to our surprise, "I am going to drop the charges against you if you will all promise to come over this fall, after deer season and work for me for one day. The fellas will be helping me saw up some wood and the girls will help my wife with some house cleaning!"

We wasted no time agreeing to his arrangement and were glad to be on our way. It was a quiet ride home.

I could go into great detail of some of the less dramatic involvements of the life of crime during those early years. I am sure I could go on to make some good excuses for why I got involved in some of the things I did. I have since then, come to realize, from my study of Psychology and living itself, that it is sometimes helpful to study the causes of why we do the things we do.

I have also learned that Psychology is often long on finding the cause, or the why of, but short on solutions to the problem.

I now firmly believe that breaking the laws of God and man, for that matter, come rather natural to all of us. But yet, though quite natural, at one and the same time very unnatural for us. For deep within every one of us, there is the feeling that we have done wrong, somehow. At the same time, we feel a powerlessness to do much about it.

That is how I felt, as the internal conflict between what I was and what I somehow knew I ought to be, became more and more intense.

It wouldn't be until years later as I made that initial step of turning my life over to Jesus Christ, that the conflict would slowly, ever so slowly, disappear.

So, in the meantime, I'd have to endure the best that I could. Stealing and getting caught, is better in the long run, than stealing and not getting caught. I didn't know that then, I thought it was the worst thing in the world to get caught.

It made me more and more insecure and unsure of myself, as I continued to move further and further away from the accepted standards.

So, by the time I was ready to enter High School, I was an emotional basket case. It should have been a very exciting time of life, but I dreaded the thought of having to go.

Though only about five feet, eight inches tall, I weighed almost two hundred pounds. So fat, I'd always wear my t-shirt swimming, trying to cover my ugly body, which I hated as well as myself.

I'd Rather Hug a Pigskin

The long bus ride to Wautoma was almost more than I could stand. I was headed for my first day of high school. I wondered what classes I should take. In those days, we registered for classes on the first day of school. "Hey, Les!" blurted out an upper classman, "Whatcha gonna take this year? Basket weaving and Art?" I couldn't help but cringe within. I wanted to bust the guy in the mouth. "No. I think I'll take football and girl watching. How about you?"

Boyd had gone to high school the year earlier, but that helped me very little, for he had always done well and was always a very good student. As we left the bus and headed for the long line already formed outside the counselor's office, I could feel the butterflies in my stomach. I was getting sick. Standing alone in that long line was a nightmare. I knew no one and tried to pretend that I couldn't care less about what was going on. The guy next to me started to tell me about his courses. I gulped, trying to look interested, I replied, "How come you are going to take all that math and science?" he responded with a long involved plan. He had to someday be a doctor with lots of money and this would be his way to get there. This made me sick inside as I remembered how I had failed math back in sixth grade and couldn't stand the subject.

I was glad that the line was long and moving slowly. I had more time to try to decide what to take. The guy asked, "What classes are you taking?" I gulped again, "I think I'll take basket weaving, girl watching and football!" He laughed and we continued talking more about his great future. I wanted to slug him, but I knew I couldn't do that. I was sick on the inside and laughing on the outside.

I was so filled with fear that I could not bear the thought of taking any course I might fail and I knew I would fail math if I took it. Standing there in line was one of the longest days of my life as I tried to figure out how I would get out of taking math, or any other class that I might fail in. I knew, deep down, that I would have to take math someday if I ever expected to graduate. But all I was thinking about was survival for this first year.

That strong feeling of unacceptability, which had been building in me for many years, all seemed to come to a head. I finally settled it with myself. I was going to put off math, which everyone was taking, and take instead, Industrial Arts, Arts and Crafts, English and typing, the easiest classes that I felt I had a pretty good chance of passing. I wasn't at all sure of that but I wanted to keep the odds as high as I could.

This was the beginning of a development of the attitude of the careless and unconcerned Les that was to characterize me throughout my school years.

I got pretty good at it too. Putting on a big front, acting like nothing bothered me. Beware when you see people that project the attitude that nothing at all bothers them. I was the biggest phony in the world, acting a part and trying to hide my true feelings.

I managed to avoid that math class until my senior year and knew then I had to take it. Boy, that was something, a senior taking basic freshman math, what a humiliation. But I bluffed my way through just like I had learned to do everything else.

"Hey, you!" the coach of the football team yelled at me the spring earlier, as I visited his class. "Are you going out for football next fall?" His voice meant business and I knew he was looking right at me. I was the biggest and fattest in the whole group. After trying to pretend I didn't hear him, he yelled a little louder, "Yes! You! Are you going out for football next fall?" I knew the right

answer obviously, was yes, so I nodded and said, "Yes, I'm planning to go out." The old butterflies started churning as I said it, but I was now committed and knew that I would have to go out. I had wanted to go out very badly and now it looked like I would be going out.

In spite of the reputation the coach had, his name even scared most of us- Mr. Batterman! His first name was Bat, and if that wasn't bad enough, his brother, whose name was Buck was the bouncer and owner of the Silver Lake Resort and Bar and he would later become the County Sheriff for an extended time. Everyone mutually hated Bat Batterman. He used to yell and scream at the players all the time and not only that, he was known to hit players, as they would come off the field after making a boo-boo.

I wanted to play bad. I would go out for the team even though I knew it would be bad. However, midsummer the news that coach Batterman had taken a job at a larger school, and would be gone by fall. I was relieved. Boyd, who wanted to play, but had refused to go out while he was coach, now decided to go out too.

As practice began that first year, I was once again filled with fear of failure and just knew that I could never last. After just one week, I was sure I could not make it. I was ready to quit, but the fear of quitting to me was more painful, so I knew I had to stick with it no matter what the cost, and it looked like it was going to cost me plenty.

One day on the practice field, big Doug Schmul, the senior center of the varsity team said, "Simonson, why don't you get tough and start giving me some practice?" I wilted and wanted to punch him out for he had been using me for a punching and blocking dummy. They put me in the center of the line against the varsity, since I was the biggest reserve they had. Now he is telling me that I'm no good. I said that I would try to get him, but wanted to quit right then and there. I didn't however, I just hit a little harder. What a mess and no way out.

Another day I recall vividly was the first time that we had a live tackling practice. It was a disaster! The coach yelled, "Okay you guys, all the first string linemen line up over here," looking right at me he yelled, "The rest of you scrubs line up over there." I made my way over there. I knew what was coming. Those big bruisers were going to run through the line. The coach continued, "First string run through and over these guys and toughen em up a little!"

"Here they come! Look out!" I could see for sure I would get killed as those big guys went right over and through us.

As if that wasn't bad enough, now the coach yells out, "Okay you guys now reverse it! Let's have the first string tackle the scrubs as they run the line!" "Oh me, oh my! What now," I sighed.

And that's how it continued every day for the first weeks of practice. It nearly killed me, but I refused to quit.

I would not quit. I don't know if it was pride, stubborn determination, stupidity, but I refused to give up. Whatever it was, I survived the season and I was relieved when it ended. At least now I would have the whole year and a summer to get ready for next year. The die was cast. I would stick with it no matter what. Whatever the cost, and it looked like it might cost me plenty. I knew deep down that my only claim to fame in high school would have to be football, for it sure wasn't going to be anything else.

I began to relax a little and got down to the business of school as the year rolled on. It was then that I met Elward. We had a typing class together and had some time to chat about school, and soon became friends. He lived on a farm near Wautoma and seemed to me to have something different about him. I could not put my finger on what it was, but I was drawn to him for some reason. One day in study hall, I suggested, " Hey Elward, let's get together a go hunting this weekend." He replied, "I'd like to Les, but I can't do that, I have to go to church, and besides, I never go hunting or fishing on Sunday." What's this, I thought to myself, a guy who is so religious he can't go hunting or fishing on Sunday. I continued thinking, "Do I want to get mixed up with a fanatic like this? If I do, people will think that I'm like him." This was the beginning of a struggle that was to continue for years. Should I be involved with this guy or not. What are people going to say? Much less, think about me.

But at any rate, we continued our school friendship and found that we had a lot in common- sports, hunting and fishing, and I guess religion. I was religious since I went to church every Sunday, whether I needed it or not. His religion seemed a lot harder than mine, and since mine was hard enough at the time, I wanted none of his. The bad part was that to me he seemed to always be talking about it and somehow pushing it on me. This put a strain on our relationship, but since I was so in need of a real friend, I overlooked this.

I had another problem with this new friend of mine. I knew that he must be what we called a "Holy Roller". My problem was that he did not fit the picture of what I had been given for the "Holy Roller". This bothered me. Yes, Elward did talk freely about the Lord, but he never hollered, or danced about it. He was very normal. This bothered me. Elward was the exact opposite. I guess they did all that in church and were taught no to do it in school. He had something I wanted and needed, what it was or how to get it, I did not know.

I finished the first year, and somehow managed to pass even the art class I had taken. The second year brought another round of the same for football. It was a disaster, with little hope except that now the big seniors were all gone, but this time the juniors took their place and at least they were not as big and by now, I was bigger myself. Bigger as is in pounds, crowding the 200-pound mark, and slow as a turtle. Early on the coach yelled, "Simonson, get in shape. Do ten extra laps today and get with it!" My thought was, "Why is everybody picking on me all the time? I'm not fat. It's not fair." I got mad and determined to make life miserable for as many as I could even if I had to sit on the bench all year.

Suddenly, mid-way through the season, I had the shock of my life. The coach yelled, "Simonson! Go in there for Mathias and be quick about it!" I almost fainted, as I jumped up off the bench and waddled out on the field. What was going to happen now, I wondered to myself. It was the break I had been waiting for, but I wasn't expecting it nor was I ready for it. Mathias had been injured the play before and now with no replacement, they send me in. From the field, I could hear the coach yell, "Come on Simonson, get tough there and hold em out! You CAN do it!" I needed that, for by now my knees were knocking so bad I was sure everyone was hearing it and looking right at me.

I had made the team and to my surprise, thanks to the injured Arden Mathias, I had a starting place on the team as a sophomore. That moved my ego up a step or two, however, I was not convinced inside that I was any good, they just did not have anyone else to put in there. That's why I got the job. I wanted to believe that I was good, but I couldn't do it.

The season ended and I once again found myself back in the classroom with books, still avoiding math, of course, but putting on that "I don't care" attitude, as usual.

Those were some painful years; even thinking about it now brings back a lot of the hurt and pain. Where we get this, I do not know. Psychology tells us that the self-image develops at a very early age. I agree with that, and mine was not good. I was a real mess.

As I walked down the hall one day between classes, Dub Schultz, a teammate hollered out, "Hey, Simm, who you taking to the dance Saturday night?" Gulp; there it was, in plain view for all the school to hear. I yelled back, " How about you, Dubbie, I'll take you, what time do you want me to pick you up?" We both let out a big laugh as we went on to the next class.

I may have been laughing on the outside, but inside I wasn't. It had touched another nerve. Yes, I wanted to date and I like girls, but it was out of the question to even think about it. I just knew that I would never be accepted by any of them, if I ever did get up the courage to ask one.

It was best not to even think about it for then I didn't have to think about what would happen if I did ask one and she refused.

One day the word was out around school that they were putting together the yearbook. I understood that they pick something to put under each senior picture. I wondered what they would come up with for me. It wasn't long in wondering. One day, in English class, I overheard Carole and Janet talking. Carole says,"Hey Janet, do you know what they picked to put under Leslie's picture?" I knew that they wanted me to hear this and I sure was interested. Janet replied, "No, what in the world did they put under his picture? I can't imagine what it would be." I had the feeling that she already knew, since she was a part of the annual staff. Carole continued, "It says, Simmy would rather hug a pigskin than anyone he knows! How about that Janet! Isn't that great, it fits Leslie just fine, doesn't it?" "That's right, it sure does fit him. He hasn't had a date in three years. Ha! Ha!" responded Janet.

I proceeded to make a big joke about the whole thing, but once again on the inside, I was being torn apart. How could I ever live this down?

By the time my junior year rolled around, I was getting a lot more confident in football, at least, if not with the girls. Of course being a football player did not hurt my popularity with the girls, at least during the football season.

My ego puffed up as Elward informed me that morning just after the season ended, "Les, I saw the paper last night, you were selected as one of the guards on the All-Conference team for the league." I replied in dismay, " I don't believe it, it couldn't be. They must've made a mistake." It was no mistake, after all hadn't we won the conference championship with a perfect defensive record? No team in the conference had scored a point on us for the whole season, and wasn't I member of that team? Of course I was, I had ended the season playing both ways and doing pretty well. I still couldn't believe that it was true until later that day, Coach Horn called a football meeting to make the official announcement and congratulate all those who had been selected for the team.

It had been a great year, even though I still could not believe that I was that good or deserving of any reward, the rest of them on the team, yes, but me, I wasn't that good. My self-image was not allowing me to accept this.

This feeling was getting some reinforcement from the following year as I found myself one of the three returning lettermen from the championship team. What a disaster it turned out to be. I saw from that experience that one player does not make a team and unfortunately for me any confidence I may have had about the ability to play football was severely tested as we went game after game in defeat after defeat. What a learning experience it turned out to be. "The thrill of victory and the agony of defeat." Having seen the extremes of both, it made a strong and lasting impression on me.

That was short lived however, and the disasters of the long losing season made that clear that the agony of defeat was stronger than the thrill of victory. I was pretty proud of Les Simonson and my championship team, but it wore off quickly as we tasted defeat.

As I take time to reflect back on that experience today, I see that the slogan, I'd rather hug a pigskin than anyone I know, given me so affectionately by the girls in my class, proved to be rather prophetic. For the pigskin turned out to be very important for me. Football taught me a lot about life, it gave me some success and an increase in my self-image, even if it was short lived.

Graduation was fast approaching and panic began to set in. What am I going to do after graduation? Sitting around the table in study hall one day, how well I remember it. Everyone was busy looking through the college catalogs and planning where to go and what to study. Old Dubbie Schultz pipes up, "What you gonna do next year Sweed?" Sweed was the nickname given to my brother and me during our high school years. I guess because we were pure Norwegians and proud of it. Dubbie continued, "I think I'm gonna join the Navy and see the world. Why don't you come along with me?" To which I shot back, "No thanks, I'll stay on dry land if you don't mind. Maybe I'll take the Air Force and become a Five Star General." I knew that was impossible, but I had to be the big talker and that's what come out. Dubbie was a lot like me in many ways, lacking in confidence and feeling pretty unacceptable about his own self, but he too did a good job of hiding his feelings. Neither one of us was ready for college. My brother had gone the year before and I knew the folks expected me to go. Yes, I would have to do something, what would it be? I had already joined the Wisconsin National Guard, mainly at the insistence of my folks. They didn't want my brother and me going to Korea to fight a war, which was still going on while I was in high school. Eight years seemed like a long time to go to a boring meeting every week. I knew the Navy was out and college was unthinkable. What was I to do?

When in doubt, don't do anything. That is what I did. Nothing. That went on for over a year and it was a rough year.

It was past midnight and I was awakened one hot summer night by the loud call of my Dad from downstairs. It was the middle of summer after graduation and all that was now behind me. Dad called out, "Boys! Get down here fast!" I knew he meant business, so I jumped out of bed and charged downstairs, wondering what was up. He continued, "I want you to get out there and tell those guys to shut up fast or I'm going to call the Sheriff!" I knew he meant it and I had better move. What was happening had happened many times before in the past few years. Several of the old gang from the football team had come out to Mt. Morris, one of the favorite hangouts of high school kids since they had and 18-year-old bar. We lived just within a stones throw from the bar. On weekends along about closing time, it was standard to hear all the noise associated with drinking and all that goes with it. Sure enough, now that I was fully awake, I heard the noise loud and clear. "Hey Sweed! Come on out and join us! We're having a great time!" There it was, the old gang calling for us to get down there. Dad was not in the mood for humor, but it was rather funny. They knew we didn't drink, which was part of the problem, for they wanted us to come and join them in their misery. The guys meant no harm, but they knew how much it got to my Dad and I guess they just couldn't resist. Boyd and I slept through it most of the time. We got out there and calmed them down and my Dad went back to bed.

Yes, the folks were hard on us as we were growing up during those years in Mt. Morris! We resented it a lot of the time, but for the most part conformed and respected them. It caused a lot of embarrassment with our peers, but in the end would prove to pay off.

We were not, however, without our rebellious moments as the years came and went. I know Boyd was more conforming than I was. I guess being older helped!

I remember well during our last years in high school when television first came out. We couldn't afford one of our own, at that time, we had two small general stores and three beer bars. We lived between two of the bars. The temptation was more than two teenaged boys could stand! Sure the bars were off limits and we knew it! But when we heard that the fights would be on, the famous Friday Night Fights, we'd sneak down and watch them. "Come on outta there and get home now!" Mom would yell through the screen door. We got a good tongue-lashing and it wouldn't be long and we'd be back down there again. A football game or other sporting event would be all it would take.

We learned early that alcohol was not much good. Yes, we had heard it plenty from the folks, no doubt about that! But more than that, we gained some first hand information by seeing what it would do to the regular patrons of the local bars.

Fights were always breaking out and wives coming and going trying to get their husbands to come home. We saw a lot of marriages go down the drain because of drinking.

But in spite of all of this, if not because of it, when I turned the legal age of 18 on September 23, 1955, I would stride into the corner bar just as big as you please and pull up a seat at the bar and announce loudly, "Gimmie a beer, Karl!"

At which time, Karl Keech, who owned the bar, was deeply involved in watching TV and the Friday Night Fights, would all but fall off his stool. He wasn't ready for it! "Are you sure you want one?!" I guess that to be the first and the last beer that I would ever buy from Karl, but I had to do it! The rebellion in me had to come out. I had to let it be known that I'd now turned 18 and could legally drink if I chose to do so. News travels fast in Mt. Morris and Mother found out soon enough. It didn't matter, I had to fly my colors.

"Train up a child in the way he should go, and when he is old he will not depart from it." That's what it says in the Bible and Mom and Dad did just that.

It wouldn't be long now and I'd be leaving that little town, and all the training. I had it in me to get away and make it on my own. I could not follow big brother or just stay around home.

There was a big world out there and I had to see it. Besides, I could not bear the thought of another day of school. So it was then that I began to figure out how to do it.

I'd wanted to join the Air Force, but they required four years and that was way too long for me. High school had been an eternity and I wasn't ready for that. "Take the Army for two!" someone said, "Just go over to the draft board at Wautoma and tell em you want to be drafted!" That sounded pretty good to me.

That is exactly what I did. Boy, would I ever be sorry. Those two years would prove to be the longest and most difficult in my entire life.

I wanted excitement all right! Excitement is what I'd get! At least the war wasn't going on. The Korean War had just ended, so, I thought my chances of going to war were slim! Little did I know! The real war was just about to start.

Now I Lay Me Down to Sleep (Or Counting Sheep?)

It was late at night when we arrived at the Emergency Room of the local hospital. Mother and Dad insisted that they take me, against my demands that it was not necessary, and that I was okay.

Waiting to see the doctor, Mother expressed her concern, "How are you going to be able to go to Germany? With your face the way it is, you'll never be able to go." I retorted, "I'll be okay, Mom, don't worry about it." I was wondering what it was that was causing the swollen lip myself, since I had not taken any drugs for an overdose, nor had I been in any fight. Mom continued to express concern, "There must be something wrong, and maybe you caught something in Colorado?" She continued, "The doctor will surely be able to tell what it is wrong." I detected a note of hope in the tone of her voice at that point, but knew she was not convinced that this would be the case.

I felt totally embarrassed by the whole thing and wanted to lie down and sleep. As I sat there waiting, I contemplated my predicament and once again thought about how to get out of going to Germany. The prospect of suicide really scared me, though I must admit I thought a lot about it and how I could do it nice and quick, without any pain. I tried however, not to think about it, and whenever it came into my mind I would try to push it aside as fast as I could.

But once again, the idea of desertion appeared more of an alternative for me as I realized that I would have to move fast since I only had a few days left before I would have to leave and make the port call in New York It looked like I'd be counting lots of sheep!

Over the hospital loudspeaker came the words, "Simonson, Leslie, report to Doctor Kjvent's office at once." This was it, I was on my way now, and should find out what the trouble was.

I was glad it was Dr. Kjvent, since I knew him from my high school days when he had taken out my appendix. He was on call and I was glad for that. "Come on in and have a seat, Leslie." Dr. Kjvent replied, "How have you been doing? It's been a while since I've seen you. I heard you were in the Army. How do you like it?" As he was talking I could see that he was examining my lip very closely. I guess trying to figure out what had caused it. We talked for quite a while and then Dr. Kjvent suggested, "Have you been pretty anxious and worried about having to leave home again and go to Germany?" To which I quickly responded, "No, not really. I think I'll make it okay, but it does seem like a long time to be gone." As he continued to talk, he began writing out a prescription and handed it to me saying, " Here, Leslie, take two of these every four hours and you should be alright in a little while." He didn't bother to tell me what they were, but I do remember the thought crossing my mind that if I took the whole bottle at once, I could finish the job quickly.

I left his office and went back home not much better off than I was before except I guess I figured that somehow I was messed up because I was fighting going to Germany on the inside of my body and it was now showing up.

If I had been able, I am sure I would have taken the pills to put an end to my problems. As I look back on that time today, I can only say that I am thankful for my early training, once again, that I got from my parents and at church and Sunday School, that gave me the knowledge of right and wrong. I knew it would be wrong to kill myself and this prevented me from going through with it. Plus, I suppose, I was just too proud and stubborn to admit that I couldn't handle my problems.

That did little, however, to help the ringing sound of the general's words, "Gentleman, you are now professional killers!"

I remember all of the sleepless nights I'd had. Counting sheep, as I tried to get to sleep. Sleep was one thing that I hadn't had much of during basic training.

I remember very well the night, midway through the first cycle of training. We were far from post and had been practicing all day on how to set up the shelter half by making it into a pup tent. It took two shelter halves together to make one small pup tent.

I'd been paired off with old A.C. Simmons. We did everything by the number and this was no exception.

"Okay, you guys, guess what!" Sergeant Gustafson yelled. "We're gonna be staying overnight right here, so you might as well make yourselves at home."

But that wasn't bad enough, staying out all night in a pup tent. I found myself getting a little sick as I considered the prospect of sleeping in that little tent with A.C.

You'd have to have grown up in Mt. Morris to understand my problem. A.C. was a black guy from Chicago. Of course, in those days, you didn't call a person black. But rather, you'd call them Negro, or worse still, Nigger, if they were not around or if you really wanted to make a guy mad.

Not only was A.C. African-American, but also he was a Catholic. I'd never seen a black man while growing up, and for that matter, I'd hardly ever seen any Catholics, certainly not this close. Being Lutheran was all I knew, and all I cared to know. I had fright and anxiety, as we got ready to bed down.

With darkness descending upon us, the day ended. We crawled in the little tents lined up so neatly in long rows out there on the Colorado Plateau. In the distance, the shadows of Pikes Peak, the Great Rocky Mountain could be seen in a majestic array of beauty.

I wasn't much interested in the beauty of the scenery, as I tossed and turned, counting sheep, all night. My values and prejudices were showing and I was restless and didn't know exactly why.

"A SNAKE! A SNAKE! GET OUTTA THERE!" I heard A.C. scream at the top of his voice. He was already out of the tent and I must have just dropped off to sleep myself.

I wasted little time to question the validity of his call. It was A.C., I knew that, he was my tent partner. "There's a snake in there! I saw it! Hurry up!" he yelled as I scrambled out of my bag.

Once out, I began to doubt the wisdom of my decision since no snake could be found anywhere. "Just like a nigger." I thought to myself. Like Amos and Andy in the movies, always afraid of their own shadows.

We made quite a duo, A.C. and me, outside, looking for that snake at 3 a.m., while the rest of the company slept through the silent night air.

We both counted a lot of sheep that night trying to get back to sleep. It was an experience I would never forget. It was but a beginning step forcing me to break out of the narrow confining prejudices I'd grown up with.

There was a day soon after when Sgt. Gustafson took sick and went off to the hospital. "All right, you guys! You cooperate with me, I'll cooperate with you!" Sgt. Medina yelled. "But if you don't cooperate with me, you gonna done had it!"

He'd just taken over the platoon that day and fear gripped me as I heard him. I liked Sgt. Gustafson. He was quiet and soft-spoken, besides he was a Norwegian. Medina was a Mexican. This shook me and compromised the little security that I had gained.

To make things worse, not long after that, First Sgt. Fox was gone. Each morning he appeared in front of the Company formation, you knew he was there. Big beer belly and all, was hanging over his belt.

Later we learned what had happened to First Sgt. Fox. He had gone AWOL himself. Took off with two 45 caliber pistols and $300.00 from the Company safe. More of my security, shot down. These were strong authority figures; having them gone made an impact on the entire Company.

Later, First Sgt. Fox was picked up by the Military Police and brought back in martin chains. He looked a lot different now as he marched in front of formation. They did this to show everyone the penalties and what would result from going AWOL.

Yes, these seemingly little occurrences caused me many restless and sleepless nights.

I guess that is why I ended up in the hospital myself about mid-way through the second eight week session. I ended up being there for 10 days with pneumonia. I had even more time on my hands to think about what I'd gotten myself into.

Of course, it all had come down upon me that day on the parade field. "Professional Killers! Killers! Killers!" The general said, I'm a killer! That means I might get killed!

It was about the only thing that I thought about those long days and longer nights.

It was October of 1956 in Wisconsin, and even though it was a bad time except for looking at the fall colors as the trees were turning, preparing for winter. It was too late for fishing, and too early for the good hunting season, I didn't feel much like doing either. I was too depressed to think about anything or anyone but myself and my problems. Nobody could know what I was going through and even if they could, they wouldn't care. They never did anyway. Yes, I had finished my basic training, which was undeniable. It now appeared, as at last, it might finish me off.

I was home alone that night when the phone rang. "Hello. Simonson's; Oh, hey Elward! What's up?" He continued, " hey Les, how about coming over this evening for a while. I'm alone and have some pictures I'd like to show you from that fishing trip we had last summer, and also a big buck I got last fall?" I responded with some interest, " Hey, that sounds okay, I'll be over later." After hanging up, I realized that I might have made a mistake, since I didn't feel at all like going out. Besides, Elward was likely to start preaching to me if I wasn't careful. I didn't need that, or so I thought.

I arrived at Elward's house and we had a good visit that evening. My mind couldn't really get into it, however, as I kept thinking of the days ahead and how I dreaded that thought.

I never told Elward that night what my thoughts were and how much I dreaded leaving. I sure did not tell him about what was going on in my mind about the general's words and that whole story. I would not have told that to anyone at that time.

It was starting to get late and as I got ready to leave, the thing that I feared most came upon me. Elward blurted out, " How about praying with me before you leave? It's going to be a long time before we can get together and the Lord can help you now more than anyone else."

There was that talk about the Lord again. When Elward talked about the Lord it was like he had a personal relationship with him. I wanted to get out of there fast, but something compelled me to stay and listen to what he had to say. Oh, how I wanted to have the kind of faith that Elward had. But I knew that was not possible. He seemed to have such a peace, even when he talked about the kinds of problems I would be facing in Germany. Could it be possible for me to have such peace and confidence, I wondered? Very haltingly, I replied, "Okay Elward, but I really can't stay very long. I gotta get going soon." I guess I expected that he would want to pray all night.

I had known Elward for almost five years and we had never prayed together before. We hunted and fished, played basketball and football together, but no praying! In fact, I had never been to his church nor had he been to mine. I had heard stories of all night prayer meetings and such at his church and I was just sure that was what he had in mind.

My prayer life was confined to the four walls of the church on Sundays and perhaps an occasional "Now I lay me down to sleep," since I'd gotten older. Prayer was reserved for church, and I was very uncomfortable, to put it mildly.

As if this wasn't bad enough, Elward began, "Will you kneel with me here, Les?" That did it. No kneeling for me. That wasn't the way to pray. We never did that. That was what I had heard the Catholics did and now I am finding out that the Pentecostals do it too. I felt trapped and could not get out of it. "Okay, Elward. I'll do it."

We both kneeled down in his living room together and Elward did the praying. I really had no words of my own and didn't know how to do it. I really have no idea what the words even were, that night. Whatever they were, I know now that I was open and the Lord somehow touched me.

Soon, it was all over and I was on my way home. I was glad when it was over and I was out of there. There seemed to be something different after that night.

It would not be until much later that I would come to understand the full impact of what had happened that night I prayed there, in Elward's living room.

How I thank God today for Elward, who never gave up on me, but rather, continued to pray for me. His life had been a constant witness to me over the years I had known him. Yes, since our first meeting as freshmen in high school in Wautoma, Wisconsin.

It was just a few days later that I found myself on my way to the airport in Milwaukee with my parents en route to New York and my ship that would take me to Germany. It wasn't long before I was on that boat for Germany, after all.

I had considered desertion, AWOL, even suicide, but always at the same time I knew I would never really be able to pull either of the alternatives off. That would have to be left for those with more guts than I had, I learned that much, if nothing else.

Philippians, Chapter 4:13, states, *"I can do all things through Christ who strengthens me"* (NKJV).[1] It was this verse that kind of jumped out at me in the weeks ahead. I can't explain how, but I am now convinced that somehow in my emptiness and openness, the Lord reached down and did, in fact, strengthen me.

One of the things that He did, which seems strange also, was giving me a strong desire to read his Word. All that I had, floating on the Atlantic Ocean, in that troop ship, was a little Gideon Bible. I opened it and literally devoured it. I had never really read the Bible before.

As I reflect on the experience now, I know what in fact was going on a little bit better, than I did then. I had no idea what was taking place. The Lord had heard the prayer of my heart and answered it. How I continue to thank God for Elward and how I thank him for staying with me for all of those years.

---

[1] Philippians 4:13.

The days rolled back rather quickly, much to my surprise. I had no idea that this was the beginning of a new life for me and that I was no longer alone. It wasn't long in coming to the realization in a rather unusual way that what was happening, to me, was very real.

It happened one day as I lay in my bunk aboard the ship. The guy above me had been laying there for some time now. I was just reading my little New Testament and enjoying it. This guy jumps off his bunk and screams at me, "What are you reading that book for? Don't you know any better than that? You dumb son of a bitch!" I got the impression very quickly that he did not like the Bible and that it made him mad to see me reading it. This, for the life of me, I could not understand.

Being the timid sort that I was and in keeping with the avoidance of violence, and not wanting to be rejected, I very quietly put the book away and kind of left it alone for some time after that. Unaware then, as I know now, that it was the prince of darkness that was trying to keep me from the Word. I must admit he did a pretty good job of it for a long time after that.

I could never stand to be laughed at or that feeling that people were making fun of me, so it was doubly hard for me to grow in my new-found faith. I wanted to be approved of by people and knew that being a religious fanatic was not the way to go to be popular. Keep it to yourself! That was the way to go and the way I would go for a long time.

That's exactly what I did as I now found myself in a strange land, thousands of miles from home, alone. It's pretty hard to hide what you are from a bunch of G.I.s. It isn't long before you find out more about each other than you ever wanted to know.

I learned very quickly that I would have to get some hassle from the guys. I didn't do any of the things that most of the guys were into then. No drinking, cursing, shacking up, or any of the like. This soon marked me as a target for attack.

First, to see if they could convert me to their sinful lives, and if that didn't work, scorn and jeering ridicule that would, unfortunately for me, once again, mark me as the "Black Sheep" of the herd.

Things became increasingly tougher as time went on and temptation was there to cop out and just lay down and go to sleep.

Somehow, however, things in my life were different now than they were before that night at Elward's house. I couldn't put my finger on it, but there seemed to be a change.

I found myself thinking less about how I could get out of the situation and more and more about what I could do with my life once I got out of the Army.

"Come on, Simmie, Let's go out and get drunk! It'll be good for you." A couple of guys laughed and poked fun while jeering. "Yeah, let's go out and find ourselves some women. That's what you really need Simmie," some wise guy chimed in. They all laughed and thought it was really funny.

As they left, I continued my letter writing, the main link with my family and friends back home. This night I was going to write to Bernie Klugeow. Bernie was the District Ranger at the Wautoma Ranger Station back home; I had gotten to know him the year before I left for the Army. He was always at all the fires in the town and I had always had a fascination with fire.

With all the time to think and try to figure out what I wanted to do with my life, I found myself thinking more and more about the possibility of becoming a forest ranger.

It appealed to me for a number of reasons. It was outdoor work. I loved hunting and fishing. I hated school and being indoors, sitting in classes wasn't for me, after all, wasn't that why I had decided to go into the Army, to get away from school?

I wouldn't need college training to become a ranger, plus the excitement of fighting forest fires really appealed to me. That settled it then, I would become a forest ranger. Bernie would surely help me get started, I thought as I wrote to him.

Life would go on in Germany and I would try to keep as low a profile as I could on my religious convictions, which wasn't at all easy. I kept busy and the days passed very slowly. I did my job the best that I could and tried to stay out of trouble.

I didn't get out much. I would be called a "Barracks Rat". At least, that's the name they're giving them today. I did become more and more involved with the Chapel program as the time passed. I even took a 10-day retreat to Bertchesgarten one year with the Chaplain.

My time of separation grew closer and closer and I was not at all sure of what I would be doing.

Then one day, I received a letter from Bernie Klugow.

"Dear Leslie,

It was good to hear from you all the way from Germany. We are always looking for help here at the station and would welcome your joining us when you get back."

This really lifted me as I continued to read,

"We don't do our hiring for the fire season until the spring, so let us know as soon as you get close to coming home."

I was due to get out the following April, and with any luck at all, I could be home before then. I really became excited and started planning for going to work fire fighting as soon as I could. I even took a couple of courses in study of how to become a forest ranger.

Things were looking up. Now I could look forward to doing something with my life. I would no longer be the "Black Sheep" of the family! I'd become a successful forest ranger and the folks would surely be proud of me.

My prayers had been answered after all. It all seemed too good to be true. I was going to make it through this terrible experience and now I would have a job and a career.

As I laid down to sleep that night, I prayed, "Now I lay me down to sleep, I pray the Lord my soul to keep, If I should die before I wake, I pray the Lord my soul to take."

I had always said that prayer before going to sleep. Mother taught me the words when I was very little. Oh, how I hated to recite it when Mom would come upstairs and hear our prayers. Now, for some reason, it meant more than ever, as I remembered that night with Elward and his prayer for me, once again.

I wished that I could pray like he did, still. But, I didn't want to ever be as religious as he was. I was sure he would become a minister one day and I would have to settle for forest ranger. That would be fine with me!

The Fire Bug Gets Caught!

"Help! Help! Fire! Fire, over here, quickly!" I screamed that day back in 1948.

Douglas began to cry as he ran toward his father, who was cutting marsh grass.

"HELP! Come quick! Dad! The haystack Is ON FIRE! Come and help us! Quick!"

By now, the flames had reached the top of the stack and as I backed away from the flames, Jack, Doug's dad, saw the flames and came running toward the spot where we stood. "Hurry up and get those old pails over there and start getting water out of the creek!" Jack shouted.

Boy, I was scared. What was going to happen? I wondered how big the trouble would be for me now. Playing with matches, again. I could tell Jack was mad as the flames rose higher and higher, I didn't know what to do.

I was 11 and Doug, 10. We should have been old enough to know better, but it was too late. This wasn't the first time that I'd been in trouble for playing with matches. It seemed as if I'd had a fascination with fire for a very long time.

"Hurry it up, boys! Keep getting water and bring it over here! QUICK!" Jack yelled again. I could see that he was mad and besides this was his winter's supply of marsh grass that he was planning to use to feed his cows. He had a right to be mad, certainly.

"Help to keep the fire from spreading over the grass boys!" he yelled.

The flames were dying down now and soon it would all be over. I dreaded that, for I knew I was to blame for the whole thing and would be sure to get it good when I got home.

Yes, I had been fascinated with fire for a long time and maybe that's why I had decided to become a forest ranger.

I had plenty of time to think about what I wanted to do with my life when I left the Army. Now, that I had just been discharged I was hoping to get a chance to go to work at the ranger station.

In February 1958, I was finally discharged. Just ten years after the big marsh fire at Jack's place. I sure hoped that they didn't check up on my past too thoroughly or I would never get the job.

But how I wanted to work as a forest ranger. I had planned and even studied and had written twice to Bernie Klugow. There wasn't much else I could do!

Now February in central Wisconsin is not exactly the high fire season. That year I recall we had about 2 feet of snow on the ground and it was cold. Things didn't look good for going to work fighting fires, at least not for a while.

I guess that is why I decided to go up to the church that particular night. I remember driving up alone. It was cold, dark and clear, the stars were shining brightly.

Our church is out in the country, alone on a high hill. I'd never really been up to the church alone before. That was a place that you went with others. I'd never been to the church alone after dark before either. Church was not normally a place that you went after dark, and not alone.

We had often gone to church as kids for Luther League meetings. I also remembered how we'd try to scare each other by climbing up in the bell tower or crossing the road out on the cemetery.

"That's funny!" I remember thinking to myself, "I should be afraid, all alone out here. But, I'm not!"

I entered the church and went right into the sanctuary. It really was a sacred and holy place reserved only for worship. We never messed around in there as children.

Now, as I knelt there at the altar, all alone, in the complete darkness, I felt a peace that I had never felt before.

All of the things around me both outside and inside that before, brought fear, for some strange reason now, didn't scare me at all. It was almost more than I could grasp.

And it was then, I guess, that I realized for the first time in my life, that I was not really alone in that church. The Lord was now with me. Thus, I was no longer afraid.

The Bible says, *"Perfect love casts out fear."* It must mean that somehow, then, this perfect love has come to me now. After all, it had been fear that had brought me to prayer just 2 years earlier, hadn't it? The General had called me a professional killer, hadn't he? Realizing that it meant that I might get killed, hadn't it?

Yes, it had been the fear of death that made me call out to the Lord when I prayed with Elward. He had really answered my prayer after all.

I now knew for the first time in my life that because of my own personal relationship with Jesus Christ, I did not have to fear death. What was that Bible verse I had learned in Sunday school? *"For God so loved the world that He gave His only son that whosoever believeth in Him shall have eternal life."* That was it. I now had eternal life.

The fear of death was no longer there and I knew it. What a wonderful feeling it was, as I knelt there that night.

I got so caught up in my excitement that I had almost forgotten why I had come up to the church that night. Now that the Lord was so real to me, I certainly could pray to Him. I wanted that job as a ranger real bad. Would it be wrong to ask Him to help me get it? I'd take the chance and ask him anyway. It couldn't hurt. I'd lose nothing if He didn't.

The words of the prayer, I don't recall. I do remember well the desire of my heart. I wanted more than anything else in the world to become a forest ranger for the State of Wisconsin.

I was feeling good about the whole experience and since it was getting cold inside the church, I thought that I'd better get out of there. It must have been close to zero degrees outside and with no heat in the church, that meant, "Brrr, Cold!"

Before I could get up to leave, a rather strange thing happened. Thoughts began appearing in my mind that I had really never experienced before.

It was as if maybe I ought to consider becoming a pastor! It seemed so natural, yet my mind was saying, "Oh, no! Not you, you'll never become a pastor! You have to be smart to become a pastor! You're dumb! You hardly made it through high school, remember?"

Yes, how well I remember that! Besides, pastors have to have 4 years of college and another 4 years of Seminary! FORGET IT!

"You'd never make it as a pastor," the thought continued. I must say, I was inclined to agree. But yet, the thought persisted, "You really ought to consider becoming a minister of my gospel."

This was the beginning of an inner struggle that would continue on for years. As I knelt there on that cold February night in 1958, there was no way that I could ever see myself as a pastor.

There had been those in the family that had suggested it, but they did that to every boy that came along, and I sure wasn't fit for that kind of work. I was the least qualified of anyone I could think of.

I couldn't even sing, after all. Everyone knows that pastors must be good singers. That was enough right there. Everyone knows that I can't sing.

It hadn't been too many years earlier, Mother had suggested that I try out for the church choir; I did, just to get her off my back.

We got there early, and Julia, the choir director, was glad to see a possible recruit. "Let's go in the living room and see how you do before anyone else gets here," she said. We did and the verdict was not long in coming. "We don't need any new members just yet. Maybe bring Leslie back a little later," she told Mother.

That settled it. The ministry was not for me. Even if it were, I'd never make it. I felt totally unqualified and unacceptable for that job.

"After all, wasn't that why I picked forest ranger for a job?" I thought. School was not my bag! I'd had enough of that already.

With that, I left the church and returned home at peace within. Confident that the Lord would help me, somehow, to get that job.

In the meantime, with all the snow on the ground, it looked like I'd better find some other work for a while. Anything would do. I needed the money to help pay for that new car I had just bought. It was the first car I'd ever owned myself, and boy, was it a nice one! A sharp 1956 Ford two-door. I even planned to get some fender skirts to dress it up a little. That would cost too.

So, when Art Keup called needing some help slitting fence posts, I took the job. It was cold, hard work and the pay was poor, but it was a job, besides, it wouldn't be long anyway.

I'd soon be working at the ranger station as soon as the snow melted and the fires started.

I was in for a big surprise that day in the woods. "Who is that guy driving in here?" Art asked as we saw the familiar forest service truck driving right up to where we were splitting fence posts. "It looks like Ralph Plowman, one of the rangers from over at the Wautoma station," I said to Art as we stopped working. "I wonder what that guy wants out here this time of year?" Art replied.

And I wondered a little about that myself as Ralph walked up to where we were. "Been looking all over for you Leslie, it looks like you found yourself a good job here!" I remember him saying.

He continued, "Are you still interested in going to work over at the ranger station?" Was I hearing right? Was he offering me a job? I'd only been home two weeks and with all the snow, I never expected it to be this soon! "Had the Lord heard and answered my prayer already?" I wondered.

"I'm ready to go to work and will start as soon as I can." I said. "We can use you right away, but what about your job here? We don't want to take you away from this," Ralph said, looking over in Art's direction. "Oh, that's okay. I can get this stuff split up anytime. Don't worry about me, Leslie, you go ahead and take that job." Art added.

"Okay then, you can come in and start next week Leslie, We'll be looking for you then," Ralph said as he got into his truck and drove off.

We went back to splitting wood. Believe it when I say I really split the wood after that. I was excited. I could not quite grasp what had happened. I really had the job I had planned for, hoping and even praying that I would get it. I hated to leave Art sitting alone to split all those fence posts, but I had to move on to bigger and better things.

Move on to bigger and better things, I did. I would be in for some big surprises over there at the ranger station. Surprises that I hadn't counted on!

The Sheepskin

"Load up the cat and plow and get on the road, South on highway 22, Les!" shouted Walt, the dispatcher. "We have a fire roaring out of control and headed for a plantation of pines! All other units are out and you'll have to handle it the best you can until I can get help your way!" he concluded. It was a spring day in 1958, my first real fire call alone since I had taken the job at the station months earlier. "I'm on my way now!" I shouted, "Call and give me exact location on the radio!" I climbed into the big truck and pulled out of the station.

I had waited for this chance for a long time and was determined to do my best. My first real fire all my own. I had spent most of the time since taking the job in the station cleaning the latrines and washing trucks. I had been getting pretty bored and had wanted to get out to some fires.

The life of a forest ranger is exciting. During the fire season in Wisconsin, you can expect several calls a day and can always count on some night work on "Mop Up" of fires already going. I envied the rangers as they roared out from the station and headed for fires throughout the five counties in central Wisconsin covered by our station.

I liked old Walt Lueick a lot. He was quiet and seemed to take everything in stride, not seeming to mind having to stay behind and take the calls that came in on fires. I got to know him the best since we spent most of the time at the station together while the other rangers were on the road.

"What's your location Truck 78?" Walt blared over the radio, as I looked for smoke from my truck. "I'm about 5 miles South of the station, just passing County Trunk K!" I responded. "Keep going! Keep a lookout for smoke off to the right, it should be near the road!" Walt ordered.

Then I spotted the fire off to my right. It was blazing out of control, and sure enough, headed for a large plantation of pines. I could feel the excitement just as I had before football games, and I liked it.

I pulled my truck into the field and jumped out, starting to off-load the cat and plow unit. This was the wrong unit for this type of fire-too slow-and all that I had on the truck was a single, small water tank on the cat. Since it was the only one we had, it would have to do.

I jumped up onto the cat and headed toward the blazing line of fire as fast as the cat would go. Just then a car pulled in behind me. It was Myron West, the district Supervisor. Myron was a man in his early sixties and not at all in good health, I knew that. "Hurry up Les! Gimmie the hose and head for the line over there by the pines!" he hollered. Remembering his heart and all, I shouted back, "Let me take the hose and you drive the cat!" I really had feared that he might drop over and die on me right there on the spot. I surely didn't want that. Not on my first fire.

"I'm okay! Let's go! Hurry a little faster, we gotta get that fire before it hits those pines!" It was almost as if he was obsessed when he first saw the fire. I was concerned and excited, but not like Myron had been that day. He had been on the forest fire service for over 30 years and knew his business. Would I be like him in thirty years? I wondered.

Myron didn't do much direct firework anymore in his job as District Supervisor. I'm sure he felt he had to help this rookie. He heard the call over the radio and knew all other units were tied up, so he came as fast as he could. In a way, I was sorry that he had come. I wanted this fire for myself. It would give me a chance to make a name for myself.

"We did it, Les!" We got this one before it hit the pines! It could have been a bad one if we hadn't!" Myron said, with a deep sigh of relief. I was just thankful that he was alive at that point.

Other units were now starting to arrive as I radioed Walt at the home station that we had the fire under control. "Stay there and mop up, truck 78! We'll call you as soon as we need you." Ordered Walt.

And it was over as fast as it began; I enjoyed every minute of it. I was ready for more of this, and looking forward to it. This was the real thing and a whole lot more exciting than cleaning up toilets and sweeping floors and washing those trucks.

As the season continued, I found myself getting to more and more fires and enjoyed every minute of it. It was an exciting year there in District #11. A few years back, I made a visit there and saw by a chart on the wall that the 1958 season had more fires by number than any year before or since.

One of those fires making up that chart on the wall had special significance to me. It had begun like most others, with a call of a marsh fire. Spring was the time when many farmers burned off their marsh grass, hoping for a better crop in the summer. "I wish I could catch the firebug who's setting those marshes on fire!" Bernie said many times, "I'd have him in jail so fast his head would swim...I hate those dirty bums!"

I understood why he hated them so much when he told me how he had almost burned to death after being trapped by a runaway marsh fire. He still had some pretty bad scars to prove it.

"This fire is North of Wild Rose, Les! Take the Ford pick-up and head on out!" Walt ordered. I headed North as fast as I could. "I think I know about where this one is." I thought to myself as I drove out as fast as I could with my red light flashing along the way.

All units are engaged now, you'll have to handle this one alone," Walt informed me over the radio. Hearing that made me feel good. I was earning the respect of the rangers now. "I'll soon get to wear a badge, too!" I thought. "I'm sending the radio plane over your way to give you a hand, Les," Walt said as I pulled up to the fire. "Let him tell you where to attack the fire and go from there!"

Doing as he instructed, I found myself getting close to the crown of the fire. It was running hot and fast, and I knew I had to knock it down, and fast, or I'd be in big trouble. The wind was driving it toward me and just behind me was a big plantation of pines. I had to stop it. I could feel myself getting excited as I tried to figure out the best course of action. In the excitement, I forgot that the truck that I was driving didn't have 4-wheel drive. Pulling off the road to run on a parallel with the fire, I began to sink into the marsh grass.

I began to panic, as I now realized the fire was headed my way, and I couldn't get away from it. "I'm buried in the marsh with the fire coming toward me!" I screamed into the radio in panic. Walt came on quickly. "Keep calm, Les. Don't panic. We'll get you out of there." He assured me. "Stay with the truck and turn the engine on full throttle with the water pump running!" he ordered. "Whatever you do, Les, don't panic and stay with the truck!" I couldn't believe how calm Walt remained. Of course, it was easy for him; he's back at the station and not out here where I am. His direction and calmness helped me to get control of the situation as I could now see the flames racing toward my truck.

Prayer wasn't standard instruction and Walt hadn't said anything about it, but I did some might fast praying when I saw those flames. They were about 20 feet high as they hit the edge of the marsh and the thick underbrush. "Lord, Help me! Show me what to do!" this was about all I had time for.

Then, I saw the plane circle above me. "At least I'm not all alone. He can't do much for me up there." I remember thinking. "What I want you to do, Les, is to take the water hose and wet down everything around you with water. Just keep wetting it down until the water's gone." Walt directed. I wasted no time in doing exactly as he said. "Once that's done, I want you to get on the side of the truck, away from the fire, and hit the ground, face down! Do you hear me?" I wasted no time in following the directives he had given me. I then heard the grinding sound from the water pump signaling a near empty tank. I cut the engine on the truck, as the flames had reached only a few feet of the truck and me. I spun around the truck and hit the ground.

I could feel the intense heat from the flames as they roared over me. "It must've worked!" I thought as my mind raced to the realization that I was still alive. The truck hadn't burned or exploded. I had no burns.

Thanks to Walt and the Lord.

True, I had lost my eyebrows, quite a bit of hair off my head and arms, but nothing more. How thankful I was that nothing worse had happened. Now I knew why Bernie hated those firebugs so much. This fire is nothing to play with.

That experience cooled me off for a while, as I realized the possible dangers involved in the work. It didn't take away any of the desire I still had to become a forest ranger.

Night work was a regular part of the job. Once the fire had been put out, the mop up began. It was dirty and hot. After fighting the fires all day, we'd stop at a big fancy eating place, like the Sky Club in Steven's Point, have a big steak dinner and then head out for hours of mop up work on the fires we had halted that day.

The mop up was a part of the job I hadn't foreseen when I looked into the job of ranger. Always coming home, late at night, dirty and stinky from smoke. It had to be done and everyone shared in the experiences so it wasn't that bad. I sure enjoyed the steaks, even if we looked a sight marching into those fancy dinner places with our smoky, dirty clothes. To say nothing of how we must've smelled.

I still wasn't a ranger, but each day brought me closer and closer to it.

I think the Lord knew I wanted to fight fires and somehow saw to it that I had plenty of chances. I was really getting caught up in the life of a forest ranger and could begin to see myself doing this for the rest of my life.

All I had to do now was keep my nose clean and see to it that I would be able to get some experience and further training that would allow me to take the Civil Service Exam. I would need to pass that exam before I was able to become a full-fledged ranger. The thought of another exam scared me. I would make it somehow, since my desire to become a ranger was strong.

One day, I remember well, riding to a fire with Bernie Klugow. Bernie was the District Ranger, the top man at the Wautoma Station. I really liked Bernie, he had helped me to get this job and I knew that he could help me become a full-time ranger, too.

"When are you going to get that Sheepskin, Les?" Bernie asked, as we drove along. "You'll need it yaw know, if you really want to make it in this business." I wondered what on earth he meant. I was clueless. "I need a Sheepskin to be a ranger?" I thought, "A Sheepskin Jacket or what?" Whatever he meant, he had my interest. Whatever it was that I needed to become a ranger, I would do.

Bernie continued, "I've always regretted not getting one myself, Les. It has hurt me and I want you to have a better time of it than I've had. Only the guys with the education get ahead in the department, these days. You have to have it if you want to get anywhere."

I got the message. I wouldn't be in need of outerwear, but a college degree. As soon as I realized that, I felt the cold chill racing up and down my spine.

Webster's Dictionary says that a sheepskin is the skin of a sheep. It also says that it is a diploma. I'd learned something that day that I wished I hadn't. Bernie was telling me that I needed a college diploma to be a forest ranger.

My emotions were mixed as I realized that my ranger work, which I had selected because I knew that college wouldn't be required, wasn't true. My boss was telling me to get a college diploma to become a ranger.

It reminded me of the story of the guy who witnesses his mother-in-law driving his new Cadillac over the edge of the cliff! Torn and mixed emotions were the experience here as well.

I know today, that the Lord had been working through Bernie when he encouraged me to go back to school. I sure didn't see that at the time. All I could see was the end of my career as a ranger. There was no way I could ever receive a college diploma. Not with my record, I was as dumb as a box of rocks!

Why did I need a degree anyway? Bernie didn't have one and look how far he had made it. I could be satisfied if I reached the height that he had. "Besides," I thought, "Ralph and Walt don't have college diplomas either. They were doing okay, weren't they?"

I resisted the whole idea of college for a long time. "I wasn't college material. After all, that's why I went into the service right out of high school. The folks thought that I should follow Boyd to the County

Teacher's College. I wanted nothing to do with that.

I was too dumb for college and no one would take me. I was sure of that. So, I went, week after week. Bernie continued to urge me to consider going on to school, and I tried to convince him and myself why I shouldn't.

It began to take the fun out of my job now. This was beginning to bother me more and more. So, as the first year passed, because of Bernie's persistence and my own intense desire to become a forest ranger, I cautiously began to consider the possibilities of entering a college program.

This would surface some new and some not-so-new problems. Money, of course, was always a good excuse. This said nothing to my deep-seated fear of failure together with my completely overwhelming sense of unacceptability.

To make matters worse, what about finding a school that would have me? Soon, this feeling was reinforced when the 2 state universities closest to home would reject me. One did offer to give me a try on "probationary terms".

"Isn't probation for criminals?" I thought, "not for new students." That did very little to bolster my already faltering ego. Things went from bad to worse. What am I to do? Give up this dream of becoming a ranger and try something else? Or do I try college and risk more failure?

Sometime during this process, I got the idea that perhaps, just maybe, I could go to the county college in Wautoma. It was a very small school, and if successful there, I could transfer to a state university, get the Sheepskin, go for the job of ranger and live happily ever after. It was a long shot, but it might work.

That was it. Settled. "I'll go to the county college at Wautoma for 2 years. Then, I'll transfer to Steven's Point and get a degree so I can take the Civil Service Exam." I told Bernie, at the station.

"That's a good idea, Les. I'm glad you decided to get back in school! You won't be sorry you did. If you stay here in Wautoma, Les," he continued, "you can work here during the summer and on weekends."

That sounded good to me. I'd be able to make some extra money and get further experience to help when I would become a ranger. I'd need all the help I could get to make it in college.

I started classes that fall. I found it to be much different, returning to school, by choice and not because I had to attend. I found that rather than finding ways to get out of doing work, I was trying to find the time to get the work done. This was a new experience for me.

There was no football at school. I would find something else to excel in. As it turned out, I found myself becoming more and more involved with classes.

One day in particular, Dr. Pursack said "You'll catch more flies with a spoon full of honey than you will with a barrel of vinegar." That was catchy and I liked it for some odd reason. It was homespun philosophy. The old, gentle man had been teaching all his life and knew a lot about people and the art of living. This was a new side of education that I'd not witnessed before.

"Hey Les, how did you do on the grades?" Russ Schultz yelled across the parking lot that morning. "I did pretty good, how about you? What did you get?" I asked. Pretty good was an understatement as I examined my grades for the first time. I never expected that I would have more A marks the first semester than I had received in four years of high school.

My first thought was that their standards were just low. Then, I remembered all of the hours of hard work I had spent on the work in and out of classes. Deep inside I knew that somehow the Lord had something to do with my successes. What was that verse? "*I can do all things through Him who strengthens me.*"

As much as I wanted to take credit for the success I had begun to experience, I knew I had to give the Lord some of the credit. It wasn't going to be easy to do that. I wanted to take all the credit for myself!

I continued to work part-time at the ranger station and kept busy with that. After the fire season was over, I got less and less time there and more and more time for school.

It was becoming exciting as time passed, I found myself enjoying it more and more. I'd been working hard, burning the midnight oil, and it was paying off.

For a guy who hated school as much as I had, it was a shock to find myself actually enjoying the process. I was only there for one purpose. Get that Sheepskin and then land a job as a ranger. That's what I wanted.

Nothing else!

Once again, my emotions were mixed. I was geared to becoming a ranger and the school was geared toward making me a teacher. Conflict ensued. What I knew for sure, I'd never become a teacher. The teaching profession would get along just fine without me. I'd go along with the game and then once I had obtained my Sheepskin, I'd split.

Besides, I was about as qualified to become a teacher, as I was to become a preacher, so I knew that there was no danger of that happening. What a laugh! Leslie Simonson becomes a teacher? Better yet a preacher! Unthinkable!

I had settled that preacher business back at the church so I didn't have to worry about that. "Yes, Russ Schultz and the rest of the guys here, they'll make good teachers. Not me, I'm going to be a ranger. That's my calling."

That was my thought pattern. It would continue for a long time as I went along with the program. They even sent us out practice teaching toward the end of the first year.

Get this, I was sent to the high school and ended up taking the Physical Education class for coach Horn, my old football coach. "Hey, guys, quiet down or you're going to be in big trouble!" I said many times during my weeks of practice teaching.

It was a different world, that of a teacher. Now I got a chance to see the other side. That was bad in a way for it made me feel guilty for all the trouble I had caused my teachers.

"If I ever became a teacher, which I was sure I wouldn't, I'd never do it that way!" I had this thought many times during my 2 years at the county college.

Before I knew it, it was all over and time for graduation. The need for teachers was great and everyone was encouraged to take a job after graduation. After all, it looked good for the school if everyone was placed soon after graduating. The school needed all the help it could get, since it was state supported and many people wanted to see it closed.

Yes, the pressure was there to take a job teaching. "What am I to do? Teach for a couple years, or go straight to state university?" I thought. "You better teach a couple of years and take summer school and night school while teaching." Mother and Dad urged.

I was still living at home and they were looking at it from the practical side. Besides, they added, "It'll cost too much to go full-time. You'd have to work part-time even if you did, and jobs are hard to find these days." "Yeah, I know that but I don't want to teach. I want to be a forest ranger!" I reminded.

So it went on and on. What to do? I guessed it wouldn't kill me to teach for a couple of years and then as soon as I get the Sheepskin, I'll get the job where I really belong.

"Mr. Simonson, please report to the principle's office at once!" the p.a. blared. "Now what did I do?" I thought as I headed to the office. "The word is out that you are taking the boys in the bathroom and spanking them with a board," Mrs. Mortenson, the principle asked. "Is that true? We can have none of this. If the parents find out about it we'd be in big trouble. You understand, don't you!" She concluded. I was furious and let her know it, "How are we supposed to get them to behave if we can't let them know who the boss is?" I asked. "So, if the parents do find out about it, that is where the problems are anyway. We need to get some of those parents in here!"

That was just the beginning of my education, and introduction to the profession of teaching. It would be six years before I finally would leave the classroom. During that time, I'd learn a lot about parents, kids and schools; how they do and do not work. I'd also learn a thing or two about myself during those six long years.

The first year had been a long one. Nothing seemed to work the way it was supposed to. It didn't work in the way they said it would, and I had resorted to the way I'd learned it in the Army and in school myself.

Along about April that first year, I resorted to making kites in class as a way of getting the student's interest. It was a big project and the day finally arrived to see if they would fly.

I had the whole class with me across the road from the school at Gard's Corner in Waupaca, where I was teaching. I saw Mr. Town, one of the school board members, drive up that morning. "Oh, no," I remember thinking, "I'm in big trouble now; out flying kites with my class when I should be in teaching!"

When I saw him coming to me, I was sure that I'd had it! "Here! I have a contract for you for next year, if you want it!" He said. "If you want to think about it, I'll be in the cafeteria until after lunch today." He concluded as he walked away. "Well, at least he didn't chew me out." I thought as I looked at the contract. My eyes widened quickly as I noticed the amount typed in the contract. $3,600.00. I looked again, in disbelief. "That's $100.00 more than I received this year." I felt like hollering out to Mr. Town as he headed for the school, "You go fly a kite, yourself! Keep your school and your teaching job!" I was so mad.

I managed to restrain thought and myself; I'd save it for later, in the cafeteria with him that afternoon! I knew I was worth more than that and after all that I'd been through the past year; wasn't about to go through that again for an additional C note.

I went into the cafeteria ready to hit him with both barrels. "I'd like to continue teaching here next year, but I need more money." I told him.

"That's the best we can do. Take it or leave it." He said bluntly.

"Don't you have a bonus for married teachers? I've got this girl that I met in college and I'm planning to marry her soon. Which means I'll need more money, How about it?" to which, he quickly returned, "Getting married huh? That's your tough luck! That's the best we can do. Take it or leave it." He rose from the table and turned to leave.

"I guess I'll have to leave it then." I snapped, handing him his contract and returned to my classroom. So I did. I was determined not to take a job for that kind of money, and besides, I needed an excuse not to teach.

I had moved quite a way from my goal of forestry. I was doing plenty of fire fighting, but an entirely different type than I'd planned at the start.

My main objective was still the Sheepskin. I knew I had some work ahead of me. I started taking summer courses and night classes as fast as I could enroll. "The quicker I can get the degree, the quicker I can get out of this teaching business and on with my real interest." This, I thought continually over the next 3 years.

I ended up talking myself into another teaching job closer to the big city of Milwaukee. At least I would be getting more money. This job in

Campbellsport paid almost $4,700.00, enough for me to afford to marry that gal I had met at the county college. If I didn't marry her soon, I'd risk losing her.

I did just that. Now, I had a wife and before I knew it, there were 3 small children coming along, one right after the other. I had not counted on that, but Sharon was a Catholic girl and birth control was out of the equation.

I didn't let that stop me. I just continued to work harder and found an extra job along the way. I'd catch myself coming back from somewhere I hadn't been during those years in Campbellsport. I'd drive a school bus in the morning before school, teach all day, then coach after school or drive bus if I wasn't coaching.

Then, I'd sandwich in a couple of night classes a week and also a Saturday morning class, if possible. What I remember of life then, it was hard to sit down, but soon, I'd have that Sheepskin.

That's really all that mattered. It would all be worth it if I could get a job as a ranger.

Finally, in August of 1964, I completed my degree at the University of Wisconsin at Oshkosh. This meant I had now taught school for four years, during which earned 2 full years of college. I was proud of myself and now could take that exam, at last.

I imagined myself back at the ranger station and the excitement. It wouldn't be long now for I was certain to get a job with all of my connections and previous work in the department. All I had left was to pass the Civil Service Exam and I was in.

"Boy, That was the toughest test I've ever taken!" I told Sharon when I arrived home after nearly five hours of testing. I was exhausted and it was going to be at least a month before the results were announced. "There was a lot of math and science, plus forestry stuff I didn't know anything about" I pondered this, and sweat it out. This exam meant more to me than any in the past 6 years since entering college.

"What'll I do if I don't make it? I don't even want to think about it!" these thoughts wrestled for weeks.

"You have a letter here from the State, Les!" Sharon said to me as I returned from school that evening. I opened the letter and read the result.

"FAIL" was written across the top of the page. I wanted to cry. The old familiar feeling had returned. "A failure, once again. I was really no good after all. All of the success I had experienced meant nothing now." What made it worse was the score. It was written across the top also.

69 $^3/_4$ points.

"Why did it have to be that? Why not 60 or 65? Even 69, would have been better. Anything but what was there.

70 points was the passing score. I was just sick from the pain. That wasn't fair. If I'd passed, since I was a veteran, I was entitled to 10 extra points. However, you had to pass in order to receive the additional points.

"Maybe they made a mistake in grading?" I said to Sharon. "They must've made a mistake, I know that I did better than that." Before the entire experience was over, I made a trip all the way to Madison to personally check over my exam, it did no good. It was all over now.

I couldn't bear the thought of going through that again, risking another fail. I wanted to cry, or get mad, or maybe even die. I couldn't cry. Men don't do that. So, whom could I get mad at?

Why did the Lord allow this to happen? Hadn't he helped me to get the job? It made no sense. I didn't need that kind of a God, I knew that much.

I had my Sheepskin, all right, but what good did it do me? That diploma was worthless to me if I couldn't be a ranger. If there were ever a cause for sorrow in my life, this did it.

A Cause for Sorrow

It was a New Year's Eve party that Sharon and I were invited to that should have been the happiest time of our lives. "Happy New Year, Les! Happy New Year, Sharon!" Frank shouted.

He was a teacher and a friend that had invited us to his home to ring in the New Year, 1965 and say goodbye to 1964. It should have been one of the happiest times of our lives. But it wasn't for me.

Sharon and I had our health, three beautiful children; Sharon had given me two healthy sons and a sweet little daughter, I had a good job. Sure we had some bills and there were things that we couldn't buy due to lack of money. After all, teachers didn't make all that much, at least not in those days.

"Come on Les, Have a drink! That'll cheer you up! This is a time to celebrate," Frank said. "No thanks, Frank," I said. I couldn't do that, people would talk and besides, I never touched the stuff. Boy, how I wanted to take that drink and several more just like it. If ever anyone had a good reason to drink, I felt I did.

I had a party of my own going. Not a New Year's Eve party either. I had a grand pity party going full swing. It had been going on for some time now. Since I received the news of that failure on the Civil Service exam. I was just sickened and had been so for some time.

I was experiencing great mental pain and uneasiness caused by that disappointment. The pain was unbearable and worsening. I had been able to hide it, for the most part, on the job. I kept busy and would be able to make it. Where it really took its toll was at home.

Sharon knew that I was disappointed, but I doubt that she ever knew to what extent. I would not let her know. For we were having further problems of our own that were a further cause for sorrow.

"You'll be sorry if you marry that girl!" Mother said. "Those Catholics never change and all your children will have to be raised Catholic." How well I remembered her words even up to the day we were married on October 28, 1961.

The wedding took place at Saint Mary's Catholic Church in Kingston, Wisconsin. It had been a hard day for me, having to go through being married in a Catholic church. Worse yet, all my Lutheran relatives had to come.

"Let's run off to Iowa and get married!" I told Sharon. We had tried to resolve our religious differences without success for almost 3 years. Sharon agreed, but at the last minute said, "I can't do it, Les. I just can't do it. Please, let me get married in my church!"

Deep down, I resented this and would carry this with me and hold it against her for a long time. That is why it is so hard now to try to share that hurt and pain with her.

The resentment gave me just the excuse I needed to make life miserable for Sharon. Misery loves company, and since she caused it, I was justified in trying to do anything to get her to see my way.

"Why don't you ever go to church anymore? You used to go all the time before we were married. You had even talked about becoming a minister." Sharon would say.

Neither of us went to church. The only time we went was after one of the kids was born and we'd have to have them baptized; in her church, of course! How I resented that! I never asked Sharon why she didn't go to her church more often. I thought she ought to go with me anyway.

Resentment is really nothing but suppressed anger. So really, I was filled with anger. My anger was towards Sharon for not being Lutheran. I had anger towards the Lord for not giving me what I wanted, and anger at myself for not standing up for what I wanted.

By not attending church, I was only letting the Lord know how angry I was at him, but I was making Sharon feel guilty.

"You got me that job as a ranger and took it away," I grumbled to the Lord. "I worked all those years to get that Sheepskin, For what! True, I'm now halfway toward the ministry, but I know you don't want me there. I'd make some kind of Lutheran minister with a Catholic wife!"

C'mon, have a drink! It's my birthday!" Sharon's Dad, Gordon, urged me. We had gone down to the tavern to pick up some more beer for the party at his home. "Okay, I'll take one," I replied. Gordon was a very heavy drinker during those days and whenever he visited, it was easy to have a few drinks.

Somehow that made it easier to have a drink now and then. I knew that it was not what I needed, but I justified it on the basis that life had dealt me a low blow, and besides, everybody else was doing it.

Sharon's parents never approved of our marriage either. Sharon was the oldest girl of seven children and it was rough for her folks when she did the unthinkable, in marrying a Lutheran. Gordon had always given me a cold shoulder, and I can't say that I blamed him. After all, I had taken away his daughter and I would be trying to take her away from his church too.

"I better drive home, Les. You're in no shape to be driving," Sharon said. "I'm okay. There's nothing wrong with me. What do you think, I'm drunk or something?" I said. We were just leaving the wedding reception of her sister, Maureen. Boy, was I sick that night! I threw up as soon as I reached our home. Everyone thought that it was hilarious that Les was loaded. I was furious about the whole situation and my pride had really been hurt.

I'd never let myself get into that shape before. "What's happening to me?" I wondered as my thoughts flashed back to that night in the church back home. I had felt the presence of the Lord in such a real way and I was certain that he was working in my life. I knew He had helped me through the Army and then, even to get the job I wanted. Where was he now?

I must admit, I hadn't bothered to ask the Lord about marrying Sharon. Maybe I had better try to make peace with the Lord. It looked like He was the only one that could help me now.

"Reverend Jacobsen stopped by this afternoon," Sharon said during dinner that night. He was the pastor of a Lutheran church we had visited a couple of weeks earlier. 'What did he want anyway?" I snapped. "Nothing really. He just wanted to pay us a visit since we had been to his church recently," She said," We talked for quite a bit, he also said something that surprised me a lot." Sharon continued, "He told me I should be going to church. He said he didn't care where I went, but that I needed to be going."

I didn't like the sound of that, at least the guy could have told her to go to a Lutheran church. "What kind of pastor was he anyway?" I wondered. "He also said he'd like to come back some evening when you were home. He wants to talk to you, too." Sharon added.

"What does he want to talk to me for? I don't have any problem." I thought. Sure enough, he did come back soon after that. We talked for quite a while. Actually, he did most of the talking. I wasn't in the mood for talking about then. Finally, he said, "Les, have you ever considered taking a Dale Carnagie course? They're good for people who have trouble talking to people." "Why? Who does this guy think he is, anyway? I should kick him in the teeth!" I thought. I was so mad, "the nerve of this guy coming into my house and saying something like that. He should be on my side. Not against me!"

I really wasn't aware of the shape I was in emotionally. All I could see was how Sharon was making life miserable for me. It was all her fault. If only she would become a Lutheran.

Those were my thoughts then, but I never would have considered expressing them. I expressed them through sulking and pouting and feeling sorry for myself. I was sullen most of the time. Sharon would be able to tell you what I was really like in those days.

Webster defines sullen in this way: "showing resentment by silence, withdrawal, etc.; gloomy; angry." That says it better than I ever could. I was full of resentment and feeling really sorry for myself. Yes, I had plenty of cause for sorrow, and I continued to carry on this elaborate pity party.

"Will you call Pastor Jacobsen and tell him I'd like to take instruction on how to become a Lutheran, Les?" Sharon said that day as we were driving home from church. We had been attending there more often now since he had been out to visit us.

I wasted no time in talking to him about the subject. This was almost more than I could grasp. Was it finally happening? It looked like I was finally getting my way. It was about time! What was that I had read somewhere in all that study, trying to prove I was right and Sharon was wrong. Yes, Luther said it, himself, "Lutheranism is for good Catholics!"

"Yes, Leslie, we have an instruction class starting next month that Sharon could get in," Reverend Jacobsen said, as we talked over the telephone, he continued, "I would like to have you take the course with her. I think it would be a good idea for both of you to go through it together."

What was this I was hearing? Me? Take the class too? Who does this guy think he is anyway? I surely don't need this class. I've already been through confirmation and all the study I've read to get Sharon straightened out! I didn't like it, but I went along with it.

It had taken 5 years and now it looked like it was all worth it. I had finally won the battle the only problem with this was that one battle does not win the war. The war was far from being over.

"Get OUT of this house and DON'T come BACK! You're not welcomed here ANYMORE!" Gordon yelled. "Sharon, you and the kids can come anytime, but your husband is not welcome here. He's the one responsible for this mess. If it wouldn't have been for him, none of this would have ever happened!" he shouted on the day we were getting ready to leave their home.

After making the decision to join the Lutheran church, Sharon had made a trip to her parents alone, to tell them about her choice. They had been broken by this news and filled with grief. Sharon's mother had asked, "Why didn't you bring the children with you? We'll never be able to see them again."

This had been so tragic for them; they feared that this might be coming for a long time. For them, her leaving the church meant that she was now cut off from the sacraments of the church and thus, cut off from salvation and eternal life; headed directly to hell!

I suppose what hurt Sharon the most was when her Mother said, "It would've been better if you had never been born. At least then, this would never have happened." This was a heavy burden for Sharon to carry.

So, it was completely understandable for them to react the way that they did toward me when we later came to visit them with the children. It was so painful. Nothing was mentioned until we got ready to leave.

I was not prepared for their reaction. It hurt them deeply, but I became very angry and defensive. "That's fine with me!" I said, "Come on Sharon, Let's get out of here!"

It would be a long time before I ever set a foot on their property again. Little did I realize at the time how much it hurt Sharon and how this day would affect her in the days that lay ahead.

Now the war wasn't over. I'd won the battle, but there would still be cause for sorrow as the days rolled on. The sorrow would turn out to be more for Sharon now, than for myself. I had been disarmed when Sharon had given in to what I wanted. I wasn't used to that and didn't know how to handle it.

I had another problem too. When Sharon joined my church, she not only took away much of my justification for the self-pity I was harboring, but it took away a major excuse I'd been using for why I couldn't become a pastor.

Now that I had a Lutheran wife, that meant I'd have to find a new excuse for not going to the Seminary. I'd think of something. After all, I still had the pain and uneasiness caused by the failure of the Civil Service exam. It wasn't Sharon's fault. The Lord was responsible for that one. I wasn't about to do anything for him. Even if I had wanted to, I couldn't afford it.

I had a wife and three children to support, and it took all I made to keep even. No, Seminary was out of the question. Besides, I didn't go to church half the time and drank and now, I even smoked. I had a thousand and one reasons why I couldn't and they were all good ones.

Les at 6 months with Dad

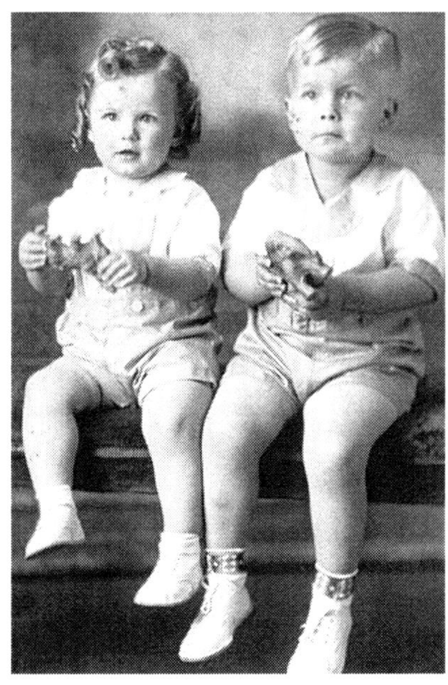

Les and brother Boyd,
Looks pretty official

Les and brother Boyd in sandbox in back yard under old cottonwood tree.

Les in 8th grade, (A soldier already)

Mount Morris Holden Lutheran Church(Baptism& Confirmation)

Church Inside.

High School Graduation picture (1955)

Les's Official Photo as
Teacher/Counselor

Birthplace, Mt. Morris, WI

High School football photo, Wautoma High School (Hornets, ConferenceChampions, 1954B

Les and Sharon

Sharon and Les after their wedding at Saint Mary's Catholic Church in Kingston, Wisconsin October, 1961

Graduation with B. S. Degree in Education from University of Wisconsin, Oshkosh, Les with Mother and Dad

Graduation with M.S. Degree in Counseling from University of Wisconsin Stout, Memomonie, WI. Les with Dad

Sharon and Les after Ordination to Ministry,
Blairsburg, Iowa United Church Of Christ,
November 3, 1974

Chapel at Camp Eschborn West Germany

Water Baptism at Camp Eschborn West Germany

Chaplain Les Simonson with Dr. Gene Neill
At Camp Eschborn West Germany

Field Service with Troops on Training Exercises in West Germany

Chaplain Les Preparing for Field Service

Chaplain Les with Chief of Chaplains Major General Matthew Zimmerman and nephew Lt Thomas Leitch at Four Chaplains Memorial Service

Chaplain Les and Wife Sharon with our first grandchild Leigh Ann Simonson

At the Chicago Marathon with son Erik just after the running of the race.

C5 Galaxy at Dover Air Force Base were we landed and took off from many times.

Official Photo for Chaplain Les Simonson

Nice catch while on leave fishing Muskies with Son
Tim in northern Wisconsin

The Simonson Family Taken at Fort Polk Louisiana before Leaving for assignment In West Germany

Chaplain Les Simonson and Wife Sharon today in retirement

United Church of Christ, Blairsburg, Iowa, where I was ordained into the ministry

Chaplain Jim Ammerman. My Official Endorser with the Chaplaincy Full Gospel Churches

Les in dress uniform after graduation from Boot Camp and ready to ship overseas, 1957.

Chaplain Les, chain of command photo at Fort McCoy WI, where he was command chaplain

Mothers Day with Mother, brother Boyd and Sister Zona at home in Mt. Morris

Pheasant hunting in Iowa

The Simonson family at the lake in Mt. Morris

Winter in Mt. Morris for Les, Boyd, Zon and Ingrid. Baby sister Ingrid is in the sled.

Les and brother Boyd still together

Ralph and Mary Kessler who challenged me to write this book

Losing in Las Vegas

"For the tenth time, Glen, sit down and shut up or you're going to the office!" I yelled, as the bell rang for classes to begin. "Sure, teach! Why don't you try and make me?" was Glen's reply.

Glen and I had been going at it for several months and it appeared as though we were coming to a showdown. "I can't let this guy go unchallenged or I'll lose control of the class," I thought as I began to walk toward Glen. I was filled with rage when I met him, "Sit down, Glen!" I yelled. "Make me, if you think you can!" he yelled as he moved toward me with a fist raised.

He meant business and so did I. The entire class was breathlessly watching every moment and I knew I had to stand him down. I ducked as Glen took a good solid poke at me. I quickly grabbed his arm and spun him swiftly into a tight hammerlock. "Boy, I'm glad I took wrestling in high school," I thought. I grabbed him by the neck and hollered, "Get moving. You're going to the office!"

I bounced him out the door and up the hallway to the principal's office. As we approached the doors, I tossed him right into Leo's office. "Here, take care of this guy. I've gone as far as I can with him. I want him kicked out of school!" I demanded.

Leo Lang was the principal of the school. He was also the superintendent, the counselor, the social worker and the nurse. He filled every position but the janitor. Sometimes, I think he did that too.

We used to joke among the teachers that Leo was really a Major in the Army and a part-time principal. He was a Major in the reserve. I was in no mood for jokes and I wanted action. He knew that I meant business, but quietly informed me that he would take care of Glen.

I left and returned to my class. It took the rest of the day to cool down. At least the class was nice and quiet the rest of the day. I went back to see Leo at the end of the day. "It's either him or me, Leo. I can't take any more of the guy. I've had it!" I told him. "Don't let him get to you, Les. He's really not that bad of a kid, just give him a little more time." He said. "I don't think you understand- I mean business. This guy is driving me crazy! I don't want him back in my class." I said firmly. "That's not possible. I'm afraid I can only keep him out 3 days." That did it. I could feel my blood boil. "Leo, you're trying to do too much around here. You need some help. This school is too big for you to handle alone." He leaned back in his chair and smiled as I said that.

"Ya! If I had more help around here, all I'd have is more trouble." He assured me. "More people, more problems." I could see that I would get nowhere with him. I might as well forget that.

Sure enough, Glen came back and I didn't leave. I did, however, become more and more frustrated.

Sure I'd been having lots of personal problems and I was very discouraged about not making it in as a ranger, but that was no excuse for my dislike of teaching so much. Maybe I wasn't cut out for this stuff. I never wanted to get into it in the first place.

I had to admit that I enjoyed working with the kids and trying to make school interesting for them. I'd wanted them to enjoy being in school, if nothing else, since I had hated it so much.

But this Glen was getting to me. I couldn't get through to him. One night, after school, Rudy, the janitor, was pushing his broom through my room. It had been a bad day and I was ventilating my frustrations to him. Rudy was the closest thing we had to a counselor in that school.

"Oh, Glen giving you trouble, huh?" He started out, "That doesn't surprise me a bit. The old man is a drunk now and running out all over the place. Besides, Glen's brother just got sent up to Green Bay for car theft last month." I listened with interest. He continued, "It wasn't too many years ago, a younger brother had burned up when he caught in a fire burning leaves. I heard tell that there was another boy too, but he died a while ago when he was helping his Dad to break up some frozen gravel loose from their ready mix hopper." I was shocked by what I was hearing from Rudy. No wonder Glen was the way he was.

"What about his Mother?" I asked. "Oh! She killed herself some time back," was his quick reply. I had a funny feeling within me and it was as if all the hate and resentment was being drained from me. I couldn't help but feel compassion for Glen. I found that I began to treat him much differently from that day on. He would be responsible for helping me to look at students from a much different perspective from then on.

"Hey Les, did you see in the Journal last night where President Johnson signed that new GI Bill into law?" Frank Jacobs, the music teacher, asked me that morning in the teacher's lounge. "No, I missed that," I said. I wasted no time in looking it up and seeing about the details.

I served my country and had always resented not getting any of the benefits. It had been stopped just before I entered in 1956. It was now 1966 and with the Vietnam thing going on, they were finally bringing it back.

As I read the article, I saw that it went back and included all veterans who served from 1955 on. "WOW!" I shouted. "That means I can finally use the bill! It's about time! I sure earned it!" I told Frank.

I wasted no time in looking around for a place to go to school. I really didn't know where to go or what to study. All I knew was that 6 years of teaching was starting to get to me and I needed a break. Besides, since it looked now like I'd have to make a career in this business, I might as well go all the way. A master's degree would give me more money and maybe even a better job. The added status wouldn't hurt either.

"Why don't you go to the seminary and study for the ministry," Sharon said when I told her about it, "You've always wanted to do that haven't you?" I laughed about it. I was in no way ready for that and didn't really consider it. I know now that I should have.

She did have a point though. I'd considered it and since she joined my church, it seemed more possible than it ever had for years.

Now with the GI Bill, the excuse about money was gone too. Oh well, I'd never make it and besides that it would take a full 4 years. That was way too much.

I put it out of my mind and settled on Psychology. They had a good program at Stout University, a nice small place and I could even get a scholarship, if lucky.

And sure enough, I did. It wasn't long and we were on our way. At the going away party, Frank said, "Les, you'll be sorry. Times are tight and you'll never be able to get back the money you'll be losing by taking off a whole year." It made sense, but I had to find out for myself.

Maybe this study of Psychology will help to make me a better teacher. I needed all the help I could get and even if it didn't, I'd get more money in the long haul, which is what I really wanted.

As we arrived at Stout, we had the sum total of $350.00 a month to live on. It was exciting and the stimulation of grad school caught on fast. This was new and exciting and I had a lot to learn about Psychology.

It wasn't long before I'd see a conflict between what I'd been taught in church and what Freud and others were theorizing. It didn't fit somehow. I'd been asking myself for some time now some of the same questions. Perhaps they were right.

It helped a little when Dr. Stevenson, himself a Lutheran minister who attended Ohio State and got his PhD in Psychology after ten years in the ministry, said in class one day, "Most of these preachers take one class in Psychology and think they know it all, then they go out and do more harm than good."

What he said made sense all right and besides I liked him a lot. He seemed so practical and down to earth.

I kept thinking of Glen. He had serious problems. I felt as though I had helped him some. Wasn't human help effective in helping people with their problems? True, his major problems had been the result of faulty training on the part of his parents.

I know something now that I didn't know then, that was the real source of my uneasiness. I was being exposed to a completely humanistic approach that deliberately excluded God from the counseling process.

I found it difficult to deal with Sigmund Freud and the hosts who followed him in his conviction that God was a projection of my father image.

I was in a class on behaviorism when the professor said, rather boastfully, "Yes, it is now possible to get anyone to do anything that we want them to do!" That would bother me for a long time.

What about free will? Hadn't the Bible even talked about that somewhere? Of course, the Bible was never mentioned and that was fine with me. I was content to go along without too many questions.

After all, most of my professors were religious. They attended the same Lutheran church that we attended. "It must be possible to mix the two. They seem to be doing it!"

Psychology was saying that man doesn't need God. What is needed is for man to get in touch with his innermost being. Man has the answers to his problems within himself, Carl Rogers told us. The job of a good counselor would be to help the person find the answer to his problem.

I had more questions than answers as graduation approached. They would have to wait for now! I would soon enter the ranks of the trained professionals. This new excitement and added status was intoxicating and would prove to be more than I could resist. The questions would have to wait for later. I had the training and the money was out there waiting to be made.

"We'll be able to pay you $11,000.00 your first year, Les. How does that sound?" Milt Rewey, coordinator at CESA #13 in Waupun, where I was to work as a counselor in pupil services team leader for the next 3 years. "That sounds okay to me," I replied, thinking of old Frank back at Campbellsport. He said I'd never make up the loss. This was almost twice as much as I made there. Frank was wrong.

Then, Milt continued, "We have some extra benefits too, like mileage allowance and an all expense paid trip to the National Convention for your profession. Rumor has it that your convention is to be held in Las Vegas this coming year. How about that, Les!" he added.

"Las Vegas? Wow! That sounds like fun, big time! I'll take the job. When do I start?" I reported.

This was far more than I had ever expected. I got right into the job and forgot about all the questions I'd been asking myself. The work was exciting. Now I would really be able to help those guys like Glen. I knew that the schools were full of Glens.

Things didn't work out quite the way that I'd planned. I found myself spending more time talking to teachers and other professionals and less time with the students. We had a lot of meetings that never seemed to settle anything. It wasn't long before the excitement and glamour wore off.

A big part of the job was public relations. That meant attending many social functions. Social drinking was a way of life and both Sharon and I found ourselves getting into it more and more. Yes, we'd continue to go to church, but then, so did everyone else we knew. It was kind of like living two lives. I was uneasy, but didn't know what to do about it. This would be mild compared to what I'd see in Las Vegas.

I had just filled my pipe and propped my feet up in my easy chair when the telephone rang. "It's Elward, Les! He wants to talk to you!" Sharon yelled from the kitchen. I wondered what he wanted as I thought to myself that it was probably something to do with religion. He always was a fanatic. Sure enough it was! "Hey, Elward! How are you doing? What's going on up your way?" I chatted. We talked on and finally he came out with it. "Les, how about you and Sharon join us next week up in Oshkosh for a special meeting? We're really looking forward to it and just know that you would enjoy it too!" Around this time I was thinking, "I bet this is some wild Pentecostal meeting and I could do without that."

I could be sure that if Elward had anything to do with it, it had to be religious. I'd done a fairly decent job of avoiding him over the past few years. He made me feel uncomfortable. "The speaker is David Wilkerson." He hadn't told me anything yet. I had never heard of the guy. Elward continued, "He has written a book called "The Cross and The Switchblade" and has done a lot of work with young people."

Well, at least we had something in common. I worked with young people too. That's about all we had in common I thought. I didn't want to go but I found myself saying that I would. I just couldn't say no to Elward.

"Get ready for a big time!" I told Sharon when I hung up. "We're going to hear a big time preacher with Elward! He and Carol will meet us in Oshkosh. It should be a real blast."

I wasn't in the mood for any preacher and certainly not a Pentecostal. I had enough problems as it was and now I was locked into going.

We went that night to hear David Wilkerson tell us his story. It was new to me and didn't fit anything I'd ever heard in my Lutheran church. It was even further away from what I had just learned in graduate school. I didn't know what to make of the whole experience.

A couple of things stood out to me that evening. At the close of the service, Wilkerson gave an invitation for young people to come forward for prayer. All at once, Elward and Carol and others around us began to pray and make strange sounds. I wanted to get out fast, but we were locked within the circle of chanting. I was sure that I had made a big mistake in coming.

Then I heard Wilkerson say something that caught my attention. Dozens of young people were going to the front in tears. "They had been after me in Hollywood to make a movie based on my book," he said, "They want Pat Boone to play me in the movie." The nerves of this guy, talking like that! Who would ever want to make a movie about your life? This guy is really on an ego trip!" He continued to talk, " I've said no mainly because Pat isn't ready to do it. He's a Christian, but living too much in the world right now, I'm praying for him to receive the Holy Spirit." He went on, "It won't be too long before Pat will be making the movie."

We got out of there as fast as we could and went home. That meeting brought back many of the questions I had in grad school. I needed some answers, but didn't know where to go for them.

It was fifteen degrees below zero when I boarded the charter flight from Madison, Wisconsin, bound for Las Vegas, Nevada. We landed a couple of hours later in Vegas and it was 88 degrees. Such a drastic temperature change that my system was put into a state of shock for several hours.

The shock also landed several from our flight in the hospital. However the climatic shock was mild compared to the cultural shock that waited. I was shocked beyond belief as I found myself hitting the casinos along the strip and losing what little money I had, it didn't take long.

"Let's take in the Danny Thomas Show tonight." The guys said. "Afterwards, we can stay around for the late show! That's when the fun begins!" Vegas is not a place that I'd like to take a young wife and growing family. They were home in Wisconsin and would never know the difference. Besides, this is a time to relax and enjoy life!

"Guys, Look at that lady over there playing the slot machines!" I commented, "She's been stuffing quarters in both of those machines for over an hour now!" I could see that she was obsessed and clearly, hooked. We left the hotel only to return several hours later to find her still at it.

It's the liquor that acts as the lubricant to keep the wheels of gambling, prostitution and crime rolling. Take it away and the whole strip would dry up overnight.

I wondered what I was doing there several times during the convention. "Sure, I'm here to attend the convention of the American Personnel and Guidance Association," I'd tell myself. "Why would they ever plan a convention in a place like Las Vegas? Who's kidding whom here?" It wasn't the convention meetings that were the focus; it was the desert night's life.

Nightlife there was plenty of. The casinos never shut their doors and didn't really start to get going until after midnight.

It was in Las Vegas that I began to get a good look at what I was becoming, or had already become. I didn't like what I saw and I knew that I had to do something about it.

I couldn't see myself spending the rest of my life playing games and pretending to be someone that I wasn't. That's one thing that I had never been very good at. It had gotten me into trouble along the way and now it was contributing to my uneasiness.

I recalled what that Wilkerson guy had said. "Pat Boone was a Christian, but living too much in the world! I wasn't Pat Boone, but I always claimed to be a Christian. Maybe that's my problem, living too much in the world. I guess it's time that I went to the Seminary." I thought as I was leaving the desert town of Las Vegas.

The funny thing about it is, just the way it happened. I cannot say that there was any planning or thought into considering this action. In fact, it was the reversal. I always carried plenty of reasons why I couldn't go.

I suppose once I stopped fighting this, inside, it all became very natural. No big deal at all. It felt as though I knew that I had to do it, so I might as well go ahead and get it over with.

Around this time, Sharon was expecting our fourth child, and so when Erik arrived on July 17th 1970, we only had two weeks to pack up all of our worldly possessions in the U-Haul and report for the first intensive course in Greek at Wartburg Seminary in Dubuque, Iowa.

I was sure that I would find the answers to all of my questions there. I wondered about all those little chapels that were scattered along the strip in Vegas! They had pricked my consciousness of morality. They seemed so out of place there. Yet, maybe not; I wondered about a lot of things there. Things that I had done or hadn't done! Now would be the time to get it all together.

Let's Hang Billy Graham

We'd been preparing for the move to Dubuque for some time now. Sharon was confident that our baby would be born by the 1st of July at the latest! She just knew this, despite all that the doctor had told her to the contrary.

The closer that the time came for leaving, the less sure I was that I had made the right decision. Sure, I had faith! That's why we were going to the seminary, wasn't it?

I had already given up my contract for the following year. Yes, I did have the GI Bill, but job prospects for part-time work looked rather poor.

I suppose that is why I'd taken the job that summer at the Pea Pack. What a life! Here I am, master's degree and all, stacking pea boxes making just about minimum wage. Real humbling!

It was 3 am that morning in July, an unusually long night in the warehouse. "Hurry Up, Les! It's time to go!" was the call from my neighbor as he ran through the door. "Go Where?" I asked half asleep. "To the hospital, where else? Sharon's ready to go and needs you right away!" he continued. I got the message and tore for home. We'd make it to Fon du Lac with just under an hour to spare before Erik was born.

Yes, it was exciting to have another son, but somehow the excitement was short lived. We'd be moving in just two weeks and had a lot to do and to think about.

Earlier that year, I had bought a new LTD station wagon. It was a beauty! Just what I'd always wanted. In the nine years that Sharon and I had been married, I'd bought a lot of new cars. In fact, you might say, I had a thing about cars.

The LTD had been car number seven in 9 years. It seems that I never got one that I was satisfied with. Besides, I loved the thrill of making a deal and getting a bargain. Now, that I finally got what I *really* wanted, I wasn't sure that I could afford to keep it.

"I'll help you out Les, and take it off your hands for you." My brother-in-law, Bryon said. "I'll trade you for my Ford and you can make it. You're going to have a tough time of it now, without a job!"

That boosted my faith a lot! I listened to him and just before we were ready to leave, I worked a deal to swap Bryon cars. That was not easy for me to do. I wasn't all that sure that we were going to make it either.

So, minus the new LTD station wagon and plus our new baby, we packed up our U-Haul and headed for Dubuque. This wouldn't be the first time that we'd packed a U-Haul. We were becoming pretty good at it. It would not be our last, either. We had a few more moves ahead of us yet! In fact, a few moves that we hadn't counted on. Our furniture, the cheap stuff we'd bought when first married, was already showing signs of being moved once too often.

It was an exciting time for my folks. Sharon's folks, on the other hand, hardly knew what to think. We spent very little time with them. I steered clear and still held onto a lot of anger towards them. I'm sure this move was very difficult for them. Their daughter is now, not only a Lutheran, headed for hell, but married to a soon-to-be Lutheran minister. What hope of her returning to the Catholic faith and salvation was all but gone? They knew that for a fallen Catholic the only salvation was the Catholic Church.

I'm certain that it weighed heavily upon them and weighed heavy upon Sharon in the months ahead. This was something that I'd not counted on in working so hard to convert her to my way!

Yes, my folks were excited, as were all the families at the home church at our congregation, St. John's Lutheran in Waupun. Since not one son had been ordained into the ministry from my home church, I looked like the best hope.

Our pastor, Ken Kohl, at Waupun was especially pleased, since we had picked his alma mater. He'd graduated almost 20 years earlier from Wartburg seminary and now one from his church would follow him.

"Would you read the Epistle Lesson for us this coming Sunday, Les?"

Reverend Kohl asked, as we were preparing to leave. "I'll be glad to do it!" I said. It was a big church and the closer the time came to doing the reading, the more nervous I became.

It was rough getting up there in front of the church. You must not make a mistake and all must be perfect. I remember reading and re-reading the lesson, trying to get it right. I even taped myself to see if it sounded okay. It wouldn't be long before I would be doing this for a living!

I'd much rather be fighting forest fires. Oh well, that was behind me now and He must know what He's doing with me. I sure hoped so!

"Everyone will pass the course as long as you do exactly as I tell you to do," Dr. Martin, the Greek professor said. I never forgot those words and made sure that I did exactly as he told me. It looked many times like I'd never make the crash course in Greek. I needed it to get in for the fall term.

"What if I don't pass? Then what do it do?" I'd say to Sharon between classes. We would be in class all day and then I'd study all night to try and keep up. The further we went, the more I fell behind.

The only good thing was that it was only five weeks long and Dr. Martin said I'd pass if I did exactly as he said. I made sure that I did, and even he had some doubts along the way of his statement. He made good on his word and sure enough, I made it through with a 'D'. That was fine with me! I'd seen lots of 'D's' in high school, but none since leaving. That scared me. What am I getting into here anyway!

Little did I know then what I had gotten myself into? At least it looked as if I'd get my chance at full-time studies in theology after all.

I still had great concerns and fears about how I'd be able to feed my family for the next 3 years. (Although it was a 4-year program, I was hopeful that I would finish in 3. After all, I was an experienced, Master's degree bearing man, and no run of the mill student!) I looked into jobs and interviewed for a position within the Dubuque school system.

It was just before the start of fall classes that I got the call. "Hello, Les. I've got good news for you," Louise Thompson, Director of Personnel at Dubuque, told me over the phone. "The board acting favorably on your interview has come up with a part-time offer with the shared time program in the Catholic schools of Dubuque. Which means you would be counseling in the Catholic Schools. We are confident with your training and background that you'd be perfect for the position. There's only one problem." My heart rose into my throat! "What is that?" I asked. The moment of silence stretched on for an eternity.

Finally, she came forward with the demand. "How attached are you to that beard of yours, Les?" Louise asked. I busted into laughter, relieved and overjoyed that it was something so simple.

Louise went on to say that the board was pleased with me, except for the beard, and if I was willing to shave it off, the job was mine.

It was a little awkward for her to request this and she was relieved to know that I wasn't planning to keep the beard. I'd not worn a beard in the past and had only acquired one during my crash course in Greek. I hardly had time to shave.

It seemed unusual; me a Lutheran, with an ex-Catholic wife, counseling in a Catholic school while attending the Lutheran seminary. Huh.

The Lord was working for us as we had taken the step of faith and come to Wartburg.

It was an unusually balmy day in Dubuque and Sharon asked if I would take the kids to do some shopping for school supplies. "You'd better get going honey, it looks like there's a storm coming up," She said. Our 3 older children, Tim, Phil and Ruth, ages 7, 6 and 5, respectively, were already outside waiting for me.

We were living in the upstairs portion of the old mansion owned by the seminary and normally used by returning missionaries. Storms never bothered me much and I paid little attention to them in

Wisconsin, however something did catch my attention as I walked down the stairs to go meet the children outside.

"Sharon, look out there!" I yelled. "The picnic table just rolled across the lawn and smashed into the garage!" I couldn't believe what I'd seen!

"The kids! The Kids! They're outside Les!" Sharon screamed. "Go and get them, quick! We need to get in the basement!"

I ran down the remaining stairs and could see all 3 of my kids standing at the door and hollering! Trying to open the door and get in. I grabbed on the door handle and pulled, nothing happened.

The pressure of the rapidly gaining storm was so intense it was impossible to open the door! The trees in the yard were bending low and I could envision my three children being sucked up into the storm.

I prayed. "Lord, Help me!" Then, pulling on the door again, it blew open as the kids were spit in on top of me. They were all crying and by this time Sharon was gathering the family as I yelled "Everybody, into the basement!" I tried shutting the door and was unsuccessful.

The twister dropped down in front of my eyes into the yard and tore out the two largest trees in the front lawn. I'll never forget! I turned and headed toward the basement and closed the door behind me. We stayed in there for a long time.

This was the beginning introduction to a new type of storm that we would experience in our new world in Iowa. We were also destined to experience some other storms, different in nature, while in Dubuque as well. Storms that would challenge and test the faith we had and that would eventually increase our faith and trust in God.

"Don't be too quick to jump into a camp, here. Take your time and look before you leap!" Dr. Poovey, our preaching professor stated. "Camp? What is he talking about?" I wondered. He went on to enlighten us on the finer points of theological education and how soon I was to learn just how much I had to learn.

He talked about the liberal and conservative positions and wanted to help us to try to be open minded and objective about the subject.

It wasn't long before I discovered that I wasn't leaning toward the beliefs that I thought I was. I considered myself a very liberal person and having just come from the public school educational system of counseling, I'd identified with the liberal position.

But this was a whole different ballgame. I could see that I would soon be in trouble if I held on to the beliefs that I'd brought with me to the seminary. The liberal camp seemed to me to be in more power and it was sure that I was leaning toward the conservative camp.

This could mean only one thing. Conflict! The one thing that I tried to avoid at all costs. How would I handle this situation?

Dr. Poovey meant well in giving us this advice. The only problem was, did we have a choice of which camp to get into and when to do it?

The year went on and courses developed, I began to see that the conservative position was basically this:

We believe that the events of the Bible happened. They happened back there, when Christ was on earth and then after He left, they just kind of stopped. As if they were no longer needed.

The liberal position, it seemed to be basically this:

The events of the Bible didn't really happen after all. They were really just legend and stories that never occurred. Nor did they happen today.

I could see a new set of storm clouds brewing. I didn't like what I saw coming. I discovered soon that the world of theology and the vast chasm between the laity and the clergy in today's church.

Pride and arrogance were rampant everywhere. Professors and students alike appeared to be intoxicated. They were not drunk on wine nor were they drunk on "the new wine". They were drunk with pride and arrogance.

This certainly wasn't true of all, but the number was large enough to be easily spotted. Perhaps this sense was magnified as when I expected just the opposite in preparation to attend the seminary.

I was sure that everyone would wear halos and sprout wings. I hadn't received mine yet, but it was why I was here!

Chapel services, which were held daily, seemed to be less a place of worship to the Lord and fellowship among students and more a place of performance. To make a good impression! This was of great concern to me too.

"Make sure you get the professors to know who you are and what you believe!" That was the scuttle around the seminary. But as the year went on, it seemed like the large statue of Luther in front of Wartburg was more like a creature from outer space than a part of the church. What I thought he stood for seemed so far from what I was hearing in classes.

Granted, I was busy, working half the time as counselor, this kept me away from school, except for classes, mostly. I had to pick up things by bits and pieces.

For example, a fellow student told me, "My advisor told me that if I don't start drinking and smoking and mixing in a bit here at seminary, I'll never make it in the Lutheran ministry!"

He was a young man. That made me furious. I didn't want to believe him, but when I'd heard the same from another fellow student, I was ready for war.

I just knew that I should have gone to Luther seminary up in Minneapolis. That's where all the Norwegians went. The Germans founded Wartburg and everyone knew that all Germans were a bunch of drunks.

At the ripe age of 34, I had my values pretty well set. True, I'd been around the past few years. Las Vegas was real to me still. Yet, I could not for the life of me see how we could be pushing the sins of the world and be able to have anything real to offer.

What about all the younger students living in the dorms with their Playboy and Penthouse magazines and Pin-ups? The faculty not only seemed to condone it, but encouraged it!

Toward the end of the first year, we finally took homiletics class. That translated, we would be able to preach sermons if we made it through. I was ready. This was what I wanted; to be able to share the Word with others.

After several weeks of preparation on that first sermon and finally gaining the privilege to preach it in Chapel, it was time to go. All that I needed was a place to preach. That turned out to be more difficult than I'd ever imagined.

My opportunity came that summer. I was given the opportunity to go into Wisconsin to preach one Sunday. I had purchased my robes with plenty of time and was anxious to put them on.

The morning that we drove up to Wisconsin, as a family was very exciting. I'll never forget thanks mainly to Erik, our youngest son. The congregation was seated and I had just walked out to the altar that sunny Sunday morning when Erik, stood and yelled out for all to hear, "Look Mommy, Look! Funny Daddy! Funny Daddy!" Everyone was embarrassed. Everyone except little Erik, that is. He'd never seen his Daddy in those funny clothes before and he let it be known. Out of the mouths of babes.

I kept thinking about that night of the special symposium on modern theology. The guest priest had gone on for 2 hours and I was troubled by what I heard. Yet more by what I'd not heard, I guess.

During the question segment, I asked him, "What is it that we in the church have to offer the world that is different?" I went on, "Different than what we are hearing in Psychology and Social Services? Do we in the church have anything unique to say?"

His reaction was surprising yet troubled me. He did not even understand my question. He asked me to restate it and then moved on to a new question from the audience. I sat there, in disbelief.

However, about a half hour had passed and one of the Lutheran professors stood and said, "I'd like to attempt to answer Les's question!" I was all ears! He went on, "To me, being a Christian means to be over in Waterloo with the black boy in jail!"

That was it? Was that all there was to it? If so, I guessed that I was in the wrong place. I had just come from there. Six years of teaching and four years of counseling.

There had to be something more to this and I was determined to find it. I thought that it was going to be here at seminary, but now I was beginning to wonder about that.

One day in particular, early into my second year, didn't help matters. Our theology professor announced authoritatively, "Let's get up a lynching party and hang Billy Graham!"

That did it! I felt certain, now, that I was in the wrong place. I had always liked Billy Graham. I wanted to get up and say something, but since he seemed to receive such strong approval from the class, I thought it best to remain silent.

He then proceeded to attack the fundamental theology and all that it stood for. This was more than I could take. I considered leaving, but that was a larger step than I was ready for. Besides, I was a Lutheran and this was a Lutheran school. I belonged here.

I began to look for teachers who were more conservative. I found one at the University of Dubuque Seminary across town. I took classes from him and was impressed. It had seemed like an oasis in the middle of the desert.

Although that did not go unnoticed. Dr. Schick, our Dean, soon confronted me. "Why are you taking all of those classes over at Dubuque with Dr. Bloesch?" He asked.

What could I say? I knew no matter what, I was in big trouble now with the Wartburg faculty. Bloesch had a reputation around Wartburg.

All of these events combined, began to take their toll. I was building a good case of the blues. Becoming more and more depressed.

Sharon took the brunt of my anger and frustrations. Her weakened condition, as a result of the move and the new baby, within the past year, sent her to be hospitalized.

Stress is caused by changes of any kind. We were going through many changes. Added together, the result is physical and or psychological illness.

"It's gall bladder trouble and it looks like we should operate right away." The Doctor announced. Which is what he did.

I had gone to visit Sharon at the hospital that night, leaving the kids with our neighbors, the Branches. The tornado warning sounded just as I entered the hospital. It was another storm. A bad one at that; all beds were moved into the hallways. I began to think of the kids alone back home. Since I couldn't leave, I said a prayer asking the Lord to protect them.

But yet, another storm was about to break on the horizon. A storm to test and challenge our faith and help it to grow. I knew that the Lord had brought me here. Why, I wasn't quite sure.

The apostle James began his letter to fellow Christians with these words:

"Dear Brothers, is your life full of difficulties and temptations? Then be happy, for when the way is rough, your patience has a chance to grow. So let it grow, and don't try to squirm out of your problems."[2]

Yes, the way was rough and I was doing just that. Trying to squirm away from my problems. How could I be happy? Where would I ever be able to find real joy?

---

[2] The Book of James, Chapter One, verses 2 and 3, The Living Bible.

A Cause for Joy

Another storm broke loose when I finally got word that my request for waiver of the internship requirement had been denied.

Internship is usually begun after 2 years at seminary. You go to a parish and practice becoming a pastor under the supervision of a local pastor.

I felt confident, perhaps over confident, before coming to the seminary that I had done a lot. The internship committee was neither impressed nor convinced!

I suppose I was trying to squirm out of the internship. I really didn't want to move my family and take the kids out of school, if I didn't have to. It looked now like I would have to!

Roger Field, the Director of Internship, visited us in our home early one evening in the start of the second year. I remember his visit well.

"We have a church up in Wisconsin that is looking for a seminary student to help out." He began. "It's about seventy-five miles over the border, they're looking for someone to teach confirmation and help with some liturgy. They really don't want anyone to preach. How about it Leslie? Would you be interested?"

He assured me, or so I thought, that it was up to me if I wanted to take the job. We talked it over, deciding not to take it.

It didn't seem like the place for us. I really didn't think I'd be gaining much if it turned out the way that Roger presented it. So, a few days later, I told him that we weren't interested.

That proved to be a mistake. Roger called me into his office one day, after class, and let me have a good tongue-lashing. He began, "I have NEVER in all of my years in the ministry seen anyone like you! You are the WORST I've ever seen and have very serious questions about you being a Lutheran minister!"

That was only the beginning. It actually began much earlier when I had turned down the offer to live in the parsonage at the Lutheran church, south of Dubuque and drive in for classes. They offered and I turned it down.

Now, by turning this offer down, I was showing signs of being a real rebel. You don't question the seminary faculty! They know what's best for you! My independent personality had blown it for me again.

It seemed like the more I'd try to convince the internship committee that I didn't need an internship; the more they became convinced that I needed one. Kind of like a Mexican standoff.

A contest in which there was no way that I could win. I would not go down without a fight, however!

I tried everything. I even went so far as to apply to other seminaries. I found that seminaries are a world all unto themselves. No way you'll ever get released from one and accepted to another without recommendations. I wasn't about to get one from Wartburg at that point.

It only made matters worse when they found out that I was looking around. They would make it abundantly clear that I was having problems there. This, of course, made me angry.

Finally, in all of this, I decided to quit. I just walked away from it all. I had no idea where I'd go or what I'd do, but the pressure was so great, and I, so stubborn, I was determined to win.

I played my last card. "I'll show them, I'll get the last word in, no matter what." I announced to Dr. Weiblen, the President of the seminary, "I'm leaving the seminary, I'm through."

I was surprised at his reply, "How do you leave, Leslie! I hope with no bitterness of any kind!" No bitterness? Hell, I was filled with bitterness and hatred. That was my reason for leaving!

I suppose what made it worse was that Dr. Weiblen seemed happy that I was leaving. I went home feeling sick.

Now, at least it was out in the open. Now the Lord could work on me. That's exactly what He did. I'd had a rough week; barely any sleep and could eat next to nothing. I was in the middle of a spiritual warfare and began to listen to the Lord.

A miracle had happened before the weekend. I knew that I'd have to go back to Dr. Weiblen, ask him to take me back and send me on an internship. This had to be a miracle; it wasn't me. I wanted to run. My pride was at stake. Going back would mean that they were right and that I was wrong. That wasn't my style. I had to win, after all, I was right! Right?

I never expected that they would take me back, which they did. However, they chose to send me to the middle of Iowa. Now, there is nothing in Central Iowa besides the corn and beans besides a handful of farmers. It has been called "the Land of Nothingness."

I can testify that that is not true! The Lord Jesus Christ is there and the Holy Spirit is there. That's what I needed! If ever I needed the Lord, I needed him now!

I wish that I could say that I'd lost all of my anger and bitterness as we packed the U-Haul again and pulled the kids from school. I had acted by faith to go back and submit.

I was like the father that brought his sick boy to Jesus. Do you remember him?

"If it is at all possible for you, take pity upon us and help us. 'If it is possible!' said Jesus. Everything is possible to one who has faith. 'I have faith!' cried the boy's father, 'help me where faith falls short.'"[3]

I had faith, which was falling short as well. I needed to be chewed out by the Lord, too. Take pity upon us Lord! Help us! He heard our prayer!

---

[3] The Book of Mark, Chapter 9, verses 22 and 23, NEV.

Markus Reitz, pastor at St. John's and my intern supervisor, was a very kind man. He, of course, had heard of me; all of the problems that I had in my past. We would not talk about that.

I could feel the defensiveness as we sat down and he went over the duties that I'd be expected to accomplish. "You'll be responsible for the youth program. I also want you to spend a lot of time at the college. We have about 200 Lutheran students there and very few of them come to church. We need to see if we can get them involved"

It was already sounding like a lot of work to me. I had questions about the wisdom of some of it, but knew that my questions were not in order here.

"I'll share the hospital and shut-in's with you. You will be preaching every other week," I hadn't expected that. "Finally, since we have an intern, we will be getting rid of our secretary, therefore, someone must do the typing. What we'll do is this, the guy who isn't preaching that week, will act as secretary and do the typing of the bulletin, etc.."

I was relieved to know that I wouldn't be doing it every week. The bulletin that is!

It looked to be a very busy year. I had to make it. How, I didn't know, but I must make it. Yes, I had faith, but it was falling way short! "If it's possible, Lord, take pity on us and help us!" This was my constant prayer.

I felt as if I were walking on eggs. Afraid that I would make a mistake and blow it; it was good for me. Humbling. I needed to be humbled.

Those first days were spent over at Grinnel College, going over the list of students. Trying to locate them, then, inviting them to church. I knew that most wouldn't even consider it, but I did the best I could.

One afternoon, I knocked on the door in a dorm near the church. "Hi! I'm Les Simonson, the intern at St. John's, how are you doing?" We had some chitchat and finally I got around to the big question. She was a senior and a bright student (Everyone knows that's the only kind they have at Grinnel!)

"How are you doing with the Lord and the church these days?" I asked. "I'm really trying to avoid It." was her quick reply. I couldn't keep from chuckling as I answered, "That's pretty hard to do right now, isn't it?"

She looked too, as we both had a good laugh, as we saw St John's church positioned directly outside her window.

That's not what she had in mind, but it was a good answer that sums up the real attitude of many young people today.

The time in Grinnel slowed me down. The past two years had been busy. Full-time student, part-time counselor, part-time life insurance salesman, then preaching on many of the weekends.

Now, I only had one job and the pace was slow. I had time to think. We only had one income now and a rather small one at that. I guess I didn't realize what a workaholic I'd become.

It was hard, but it was good for me. There was time to pause and reflect on the things I'd been exposed to at seminary. I left the seminary behind, but not the feelings. They came with me.

I was feeling hurt and angry. I viewed Markus as a part of the seminary faculty, which of course he was, so, understandably, I was very distrustful of him. I'm sure it showed.

He felt it his duty to help me better understand Lutheran theology and yet, at the same time, work with me in the church. His final report surmised, I believe, his feeling, "As far as I could tell, Leslie had serious problems understanding Lutheran theology, and when he did give evidence of understanding it, he more often than not either disagreed with it or expressed reservations concerning it."

That says it well. I suppose what was unfolding during our discussions was just that. I slowly became aware that I did not agree with and had serious reservations with Lutheran theology.

This would not be an easy time for me. I had been a Lutheran all of my life! I had always believed what my church had taught. I never really ever questioned it. After all, I worked overtime for several years to convert Sharon.

I was the guy when asked, what he believes, replies, "I believe what my church teaches." When asked, "What does your church teach?" Replies, "Why, what I believe, of course."

After what I'd gone through at the seminary the past couple of years, if I hadn't been that tied to the Lutheran church, I'd have been gone a long time earlier.

Well- There I was. After a few months, I did begin to relax a little. I suppose the turning point came that day, during one of our many heated discussions.

We'd been talking about conversion and Billy Graham and how one becomes a Christian. Marcus said, "Really, the only thing, in fact the best thing we can tell our people is this, ' You are Christians, now act like it.'" Meaning, of course, that one becomes a Christian at baptism.

It was if the light had been turned on. After that day, I had very serious doubts about ever becoming a Lutheran minister. As much as I had wanted to, I could no longer believe that.

Maybe, just maybe, that is why one of my professors noted on one of my papers that I was a Baptist. I'd been furious at that time, but now it began to make more sense.

This was a huge step for me. One step that I'd make very slowly. I'd been hearing rumors about the pastor over at the local Baptist College. "This guy is really on fire for the Lord. He's undergone some new spiritual experience that's transformed him and his congregation," one student explained.

I wondered about that. Then I met a Chemistry teacher, a Presbyterian himself, who'd been attending his church and even teaching a study. This was more than I could grasp. It was intriguing and made me even more curious. I was looking for something. I hadn't found it at seminary. "What would it hurt to talk to this guy?" Marcus wouldn't approve, I knew that. I called him anyway one day. "Hello, Pastor Shively. I'm the intern at St. John's Lutheran, just down the street. I'd like to come over and talk to you sometime soon about baptism and your church!" I heard nothing on the other end. He had to be in shock. You don't get calls like that every day.

He finally responded, " I'm really busy right now, wouldn't be able to see you until after Christmas."

I thought he'd be anxious to see me. I guess he needed time to recover. Really, I'm sure now that the Lord was in on it. He wanted me to get a little more spiritual hunger before feeding time.

During this time, and prior to it, I preached every other week. This was taking its toll. I knew I was fast running out of things to say. Marcus said one day, "You know, Les, you're much freer in the pulpit than I am."

I had to admit, he wasn't very free. Since he'd been doing it for fifteen years, I wondered about that since he seemed so bound to his typed manuscript. Then I'd think about what I'd heard. "The only reason that we agreed to get an intern was so that we'd be able to hear somebody else preach."

No, I was far from free, that I knew. I lacked the power I needed and wanted to stand up and tell people about the Lord Jesus Christ.

Besides, I kept thinking about the Seminary and my future. All the anger and bitterness was still there. How could I stand up and tell others about the love of Christ when I was filled with hate myself?

"You mean you actually went up to the altar of an Assemblies of God church, and asked them to pray for you?" I asked Hugh Shively when we finally got together. He told me about what had been happening in his life spiritually after we talked at length about baptism.

We talked for over two hours. I was eating it up. The Holy Spirit was at work and something in me began to say this is it! This is what you need!

Something happened to Hugh just 3 years earlier as a result of that trip to the altar. I didn't want to go to an Assemblies of God altar. That may have been fine for him, but not for me!

That church was on my off limits list; too much emotionalism. I wasn't ready for that.

Hugh continued, "It was the greatest day of my life, next to the day that I received Jesus Christ as my personal savior. It turned me around spiritually and gave me the ability to witness."

Power to witness. That's what I need. Yes, he said that he spoke in a language he never learned or heard before and had been healed of a back injury that he had for several years.

I didn't have that, but I needed the power! Reflecting back on that meeting, I felt a little like old Nicodemus must've felt going to Jesus that night. I'm sure he went under the cover of the night as to not be seen. I didn't want to be seen either.

Here we have a Lutheran intern sneaking over to talk to a Baptist preacher about an experience he had in an Assemblies of God church.

The Lord has to have a great sense of humor as he contends with all of our stupidity and foolishness.

I went away that day loaded down with books and tapes borrowed from Hugh. One book I couldn't wait to read was *A New Song* by Pat Boone. When I saw it, my mind immediately went back to the night when David Wilkerson spoke about Pat. I had to read that book.

It blessed me and I wanted more. Hugh prayed with me before I left. I continued to pray more for myself and study the books he gave me. I was very cautious and checked everything by the Bible as I went along.

It was late Friday afternoon, the second week of February. I sat alone in my office trying to put the finishing touches on Sunday's sermon. Everyone was gone now. For some reason, I couldn't seem to get the sermon finished.

Off and on all week I had been reading and studying one of the books Hugh had given me. It was a theological study by Dr. Howard Erwin, himself a noted theologian.

He was saying the same thing Dr. Poovey said, back at Wartburg seminary. The conservatives take the position that those things in the Bible happened back then, but they don't happen today. I thought that's where I was! The liberals, they say that not only don't things happen today; they didn't happen back then either.

Dr. Erwin said that most churches and seminaries take one position or the other. "There is another group, a minority to be sure," he went on, "this group believes that the miracles happened back then, just as recorded and they happen today also."

He challenged me to take a stand. Where would I stand? It was if I had to take a position no matter what the outcome.

I felt myself being drawn into the church to pray. This wasn't my normal practice; in fact, my prayer life had been very poor at that point. Yes, I prayed at church services and that was about all. I had a 6-pack of beer around the house at all times. I had to have it to relax. I'd been losing contact with the Lord and needed to get it back.

It was so quiet and peaceful in the church. I took my Bible with me and now began to leaf through it. I had a flash back to many years earlier at the altar in Mt. Morris, where I first felt the call of the Lord.

Lots of water over the dam since then; running like Jonah. Perhaps my whale was the seminary! All those feelings of rejection, anger and bitterness surfaced and I saw what a phony I was.

What about Sharon and how I'd hurt her too! Forcing her to join my church. How miserable I'd made her life and now the folks too!

Trying to preach and serve the Lord like this. My eyes fell on the First Letter to the Corinthians, 14:1, "*Make love your aim, and earnestly desire the spiritual gifts.*"[4] Yes, I was aiming for love. Lord give me that kind of desire!

Whatever it takes, Lord, I want to serve you! Help me Lord! Help me love and forgive. Those men at the seminary, Sharon and her folks, let me forgive them.

I'll do whatever you want and go wherever you want me! I need your spiritual power. Power to preach and tell others of Your love. Power to love and forgive. I can't do it on my own anymore, Lord!

"Would you be willing to give up the Lutheran church?" I seemed to hear going through my mind about then. It shocked my senses! Give up the Lutheran church. I don't get it. Oh well, it doesn't matter. "Yes, Lord! I'll give up the Lutheran church. I'll give up anything- everything! Just give me your love and joy and peace, with this power to preach for You!"

I continued to read the chapter until reaching verse 12. It jumped off the page at me!

"So, with yourselves; since you are eager for manifestations of the spirit, strive to excel in building up the church."[5]

It was speaking directly to me now! I am eager for the spirit. It had to be for the right purpose. Building up the church! Not for me, but for the Lord. Power for witness. How could I have missed it?

I began to feel something on the inside. It was something that I'd never felt before. I glanced at verse 13.

---

[4] 1st Corinthians, Chapter 14, verse 1, NEV.

[5] Ibid., verse 12.

"Therefore, he who speaks in a tongue should pray for the power to interpret."[6]

I was being called to decide. Decide for or against the Word and the Holy Spirit with all the gifts. What had Dr. Erwin said? "This group believes that the miracles happened back then, just as recorded, and they happen today also."

Would I believe or wouldn't I? I believe, Lord! I believe, Lord! Help my disbelief! I had an amazing feeling come over me as I said to the Lord, "I want you, Lord. I believe your Word and I will even take speaking in tongues!"

He wasted no time in answering my prayer. I heard sounds coming from my mouth that I had never heard before! I knew exactly what it was and it thrilled me as I realized that it was a miracle and, yes, they do happen today.

I wish I could more fully describe what had happened to me. I was filled with a joy unspeakable. Yes, it was a cause for rejoicing and a cause for joy.

Webster's defines joy: the emotion of great delight or happiness caused by something good or satisfying. It was all that and more!

I stayed at the altar for more than an hour praying and singing. I did not want to leave and yet, I couldn't wait to get home to share with Sharon what had happened.

Somehow, I just knew that the Lord was with me in a new way. A way He'd never been with me before. Like the war was now over. Peace had come. It had come to stay and I'd never be the same again.

Yes, something good and pure and satisfying had happened. I wanted to tell Sharon how much I loved her and how sorry I was for all the hurt that I had caused her. I wanted to tell Marcus what had happened. I had to tell him! How could I? He'll never understand! "Please, You'll have to help me, Lord!"

---

[6] Ibid., verse 13.

No Longer a Lutheran

Pastor Reitz walked into the church early that morning. I had arrived before him and I knew that this was the time. "Good morning, Mark. Say, I've been meaning to ask you, are you going to let me go to that conference on the Holy Spirit with Hugh Shivley next month?" I'd been asking him about this for some time now, and he'd been putting me off for some reason. I continued, "I need to know one way or the other so I can tell him. He's got to send in the reservation this week."

Marcus was in an unusually good mood that morning, and as I finished he smiled and said, "I don't think I'd better let you go to that meeting. If I do, you're liable to come back speaking in tongues!"

There it was, an opportunity to tell Mark what had happened to me a few weeks earlier, right at the altar of his own church, at that. Almost before I knew what I was saying it came out. "Oh, there's no danger of that happening Mark, I already do speak in tongues!"

There was no smile left on Mark's face as I finished. In fact, he wasted little time in exiting my office and heading for his, slamming the door behind him. He was hopping mad and I knew it. It was obvious he didn't want to discuss the subject any further.

I had a sinking feeling in my gut and it hurt me deeply. At least it was out in the open now. I had been concerned about that ever since that night that I'd received the Holy Spirit and the gift of tongues.

In fact, I'd been praying that the Lord would give me the right opportunity to tell Markus. He had done that, but now that it was out, I didn't know what would happen next.

Somehow it was different now. Kind of hard to explain, but it was okay. No matter what happened, the Lord would take care of it.

"I don't want to be responsible for leading you in the wrong direction. If you go to that meeting you could get messed up in that Charismatic business and you don't need that!" Mark told me earlier, when I had asked about going to the conference.

I found it hard to talk to Mark for a number of reasons. Mostly, I guess, because I had some bad feelings toward the seminary before coming there. I was sure the seminary told him of my theology and that I was very conservative. I knew that they could not have told him of my involvement in the Charismatic movement since up until that time I was not involved in it.

In fact, I would learn later, he called the seminary and asked them why they had not told him of my involvement. This call was soon to prompt a meeting with the faculty at the seminary and myself.

It came soon after our conversation, in the form of a letter. "You are being requested to return to Wartburg for a meeting with the faculty," the letter stated. No reason was given for the meeting. I was left to guess about that. It did say, however, that I would be paid for the expenses of my trip.

My relationship with Mark became very strained. We talked very little from then on. I tried to be understanding about the feelings I knew that he was experiencing. It was not easy.

The neat thing about the days that followed was that now there was a different attitude toward everything. Yes, the same problems would come up. I'd still get mad at times and felt hurt, but there was a new peace and joy I'd never known before.

It had been a long haul. Looking for peace and contentment had been a life long struggle up to this point. Ever since that night back at Mt.

Morris at the church, I'd heard the Lord calling me into his service.

I had not wanted to answer the call. Finally, I responded and now I found peace and joy. I knew that the Lord had something for me to do. What it was, I didn't know, but that would come in time.

Mark assessed my needs a little differently, as he wrote his final report, "Leslie needs to find himself theologically and personally. Uncertainty in both respects made for a confusing internship and offered little basis for help to him during his internship."

It was true; I came to Grinnel in search of something. Yes, I had a lot of uncertainty in both. I'd say I really found myself personally when I found myself theologically.

It was Friday afternoon in February. All of the uncertainty was gone. I know that it sounds impossible. I can't even believe it. But it happened just that way.

Oh yes, we did return to the seminary for the all-important meeting. It was a rather strange conference. No agenda, just questions, general questions.

I had been impressed within to tell them I no longer planned to seek a Lutheran ordination. It just seemed so natural now. I knew it would be tough since so many were counting on me. I hated to let them down. I knew I must submit to the Spirit and His leading.

"I'm not planning to seek ordination in the Lutheran church." I announced. "I would like to continue on at the seminary and complete my degree since I have only once semester left." I requested.

"You will have to take summer school, and you've lost your housing at seminary, since you failed to apply in writing to hold it." was the reply. No assurance I'd be able to continue.

I should have guessed that there was trouble ahead with that response, but I never really worried about it. What amazed me during and after the meeting was the way in which I reacted toward the faculty. I knew that something was different. I just knew it. "Had the Lord really answered my prayer? Had He given me love for these men?"

As the meeting was drawing to a close, it was obvious the issue of what had happened a few weeks earlier was not coming up. Had Marcus not told them? I had to say something! "I must tell you about an experience I've had while in Grinnel. A deeper experience with the Person of the Holy Spirit." I deliberately omitted saying anything about the gift of tongues. I just knew better.

The reaction came quick! Fast and furious the questions came, from all sides. I listened and then tried to respond to them one at a time. "What do you mean by the Holy Spirit? How would you handle this subject in church? We all believe in the Holy Spirit, What do you mean?" Finally, Dr. Griffen, the seminary psychiatrist, asked, "Why did you bring this subject up, Leslie? I've been trying to figure out for the last 20 minutes why you brought this up."

I wanted to say to him that the Holy Spirit has led me to share this with you, but I just knew for sure they'd think I was completely crazy. There was really no other answer. But then, I guess, at that point no answer would have satisfied.

It was just the beginning. There would be no other meetings or questions along the way. Somehow, I knew that, but it didn't matter now. The uncertainty, confusion and yes, even the anger and bitterness were gone.

Back in Grinnel, a few weeks later, I had another surprise in store for me. Whatever it had been that happened to me was beginning to show.

"I finished reading that book you gave me, Les. The one by Mr. Boone!" Norm Anderson, my handball and running partner over the past several months, announced one morning. "The experience he talks about having received! Have you received it?" He asked. "Yes, I have Norm, just a couple of months ago right here in Grinnel," I told him. "I thought so, I knew something had happened to you!"

It even began to affect my physical activities. As I reflected, I realized that I'd been beating him more and more at handball lately.

Wow! I hadn't even said anything and he was able to see a difference! That was remarkable! I'd better start to watch myself!

It wasn't long before the word was out and it spread more and more. I wanted to share so much with the church, but knew that I had to keep quiet. That was going to be tough for me to do.

I had sought for power to preach the word. It was beginning to happen. "Les, you must be getting used to the public address system! You're coming through so much clearer now than when you first came!" a member of the congregation commented one Sunday.

Another faithful Lutheran observed, "When you first began preaching I wasn't convinced you really believed what you were saying. However, before the year was over, I knew that you believed it."

More surprises. Back in Grinnel, another was in store. It was obvious that what had changed within me was showing. I thought that my efforts to keep it down were fair, but once again Mark's report told the story, "On the rank-and-file membership he ended his internship the last months by appearing to call only on those whom he felt might influence in regard to the Charismatic movement."

Then again he observed, " By the time his internship was over it was clear that his priority was his involvement in the Charismatic movement. Anything else was secondary, if it rated any priority at all."

I saw the report before I left that spring. I knew that and so did Mark. That never happened. I wouldn't see it for months later. I placed it in the hands of the Lord. I knew that He could handle it.

In June, we moved back to Dubuque, enrolled in summer session and waited. Just at the end of the summer, the Lord opened a door for a job in counseling at the East Dubuque High School just across the river in Illinois. It would work out fine.

We prayed for a house that would allow the kids to stay in the same school they'd attended before leaving. That also worked out.

Then it happened! "Didn't anyone contact you today?" Dr. Schick, the academic dean had asked as I showed up in his office late that day to register for the fall term. " You are no longer a student at Wartburg."

"Was I hearing correctly? This could not be happening!" It took me by complete surprise.

"Someone should have told you!" exclaimed Dean Schick. " A resolution was passed this morning by a special faculty agreement. You have been discontinued as a student."

I felt the anger flooding back. No, that wasn't the way, something told me. Love and forgive! That's what happened. I guess what really surprised me was the way that I reacted.

Somehow, I just knew it would all work out but I had no idea how at that point. I asked Dean Schick, "Do you have something in writing to this effect?" Without question, he produced a copy of the resolution, signed and dated.

As I walked out of the seminary and got into my car, I started talking to the Lord. He was all that I had now. I knew that it was just He and I. "What do I do now? Where do I go from here?"

Come With Me! See What I Can Do!

I hadn't expected such a quick answer. It was clearly the Lord and he was speaking directly to me.

"Come with me! See what I can do!" It made me think back over the years. All of the running, searching, planning, trying to get the Lord to see things my way. Like, "Okay Lord, Come along with me and see what I can do!"

Yes, I had done plenty of that. What was the verse? "*I can do all things through Christ who strengthens me.*"[7] He had seen me through a lot. Had I forgotten that He was the one who'd given me the strength to go as far as I had? Maybe I had.

"You've got my attention, Lord" I said. I got a very strong impression that I should drive across town to Dubuque seminary. "That makes no sense at all! It's almost 5 o'clock now, everyone will be gone, and besides, what would I do? I guess I could go and speak with Dr. Bloesch. He'll listen to me. I can cry on his shoulder."

I'd never been as interested as I was now to listening to the Lord. It's not every day I get kicked out of the seminary. "If I wanted to see what the Lord could do, I'd have to come with Him."

---

[7] Phillipians Chapter 4, verse 13 NKJV

I was afraid of this. Dr. Bloesch had left for the day. Now what? How about Dr. Towner? Go see if he'll take you in. No way! He's not about to consider it. Find out for yourself! I fought this battle for some time and finally obeyed. "I just know he won't be in and even if he is, he'll laugh me out of his office. I don't need that!

Much to my surprise, Dean Towner was in. Everyone else was gone. Walking into his office that night, I said, "Say, Dr. Towner! I was just thrown out of Wartburg seminary! I really feel that the Lord wants me to finish my degree. Would you consider taking me in here?"

"Are you sure you're through at Wartburg?" he replied. "Yes, there's no doubt about it, I'm through." I said, pulling the decision out of my pocket.

Just a few minutes earlier I'd asked Dean Schick for a letter and now I'm showing it to Dean Towner. He looked over the document carefully and said, " Sit down, we'll see what we can do for you."

Wow! This had to be the Lord in action. I couldn't have done that myself if I had tried. That had been my problem all along, trying to do and getting the Lord to agree with me.

Things were going to be different from now on. This was only the beginning. The Lord has just shown me what He could do. It always is.

However the condition for seeing it is not. "Come with me!" the Lord said. That was scary. I was beginning to learn what it meant and how it worked. After all, it hadn't been that long, or had it? It was 1973! I'd met him in 1956 and that's less than 20 years. Oh well, perhaps I was a slow learner!

A Proverb keeps going through my mind. "*A man's mind plans his way but the* L*ORD directs his steps.*"[8] I had it here for a long time, but somehow it now took on new meaning. I saw something I hadn't seen before. I plan, the Lord directs! The more that I plan, the harder for the Lord to direct my steps. The Lord knows! I've done plenty of planning. I think I'm finally getting it Lord. The less planning that I do, the easier it will be for you to direct my steps. I promise to try Lord, although I have a feeling it won't be easy.

Some call this walking in the Sprit. Whatever it is, I was just taking my first steps.

---

[8] The Book of Proverbs, Chapter 16, Verse 9, NIV.

Then I remembered reading somewhere about discipleship.

"Discipleship is not limited to what you can comprehend-it must transcend all comprehension, plunge into the deep waters beyond your own comprehension, and I will help you to comprehend even as I do. Bewilderment is the true comprehension. Not to know where you are going is the true knowledge."[9]

Okay Lord, I've plunged. Help me!

If not to know where you're going is true knowledge, then I'm pretty smart! I have no idea where I'm going Lord. Instruct me and lead me, Lord!

I left it at that and got on with the business of adjusting to a new school. The United Presbyterian Church runs Dubuque Seminary. I had classes there before. Dr. Blosch, my favorite professor, was there so I had friends. That helped me.

I was accepted and told that I would be required to spend one year in residency. They would accept my credits from Wartburg.

They suggested that I begin looking around for a church, since I was no longer a Lutheran. I agreed but knew not where to begin. In fact, after what I had been through the past years, I wasn't exactly sure I wanted to get into any; at least not for a while.

I was bewildered. I didn't know where I was going. It was different than before. Everything was different. The peace was there and so was the joy. "Lead me Lord! Please show me what you want me to do!"

The Lord wasted little time in doing just that.

"Hello, Les! This is Steve Heetland from Wartburg. I heard that you've left the seminary. Sorry to hear that! What are you doing now?" Steve had called me from his church in southern Iowa. He'd graduated the year earlier and taken on that church. "It's great out here, Les! I'm having a good ministry. I've been in the reserve too, as a chaplain. Have you ever thought about the chaplaincy, Les?" "No, I can't say that I have. I'm too old for that anyway. Besides, the Army is not for me." I told Steve.

I wondered about that call. Steve and I hadn't been that close. Yes, He was concerned. Oh well!

---

[9] *The Cost of Discipleship:* Dietrich Bonhoeffer.

Not long after that, I went to a conference held for pastors and seminary students. Another student and myself sat at a table at a nearby restaurant. This guy walks up to our table and announces, "Say, have either of you gentleman ever considered becoming an Army chaplain?"

I assured him, I had not. My friend was not quite so sure. At once I thought about the call from Steve. No, couldn't be! Just a coincidence!

Sure, I wanted to be open to the Lord's leading, Sure, I'd prayed, "Show me what you want me to do!" The Army was one place that I was sure the Lord didn't want me!

I went home and tried to forget the whole thing. The strong feeling would not leave! "Come with me and see what I can do! I want you to consider the chaplaincy!"

The chaplaincy was one thing that I had never considered before. I'd considered a lot of other things but not that. The more that I did think about that, the more I wondered why I hadn't, in fact, ever considered it.

It didn't take me long to figure that one out! I hated the Army! It had cost me the two most miserable years of my life! That's why! Sure, they need chaplains in the Army. I'm way too old anyway! You don't want me to consider the chaplaincy, do you Lord?"

Sure, Sharon and I knew that we would have to go to the Lord for direction. We'd known that for a long time and we'd done it. Now things were beginning to look somewhat different.

We were praying together now! That had not been our practice. Most of our praying had been along the lines of "Lord! Help me and get this thing or that problem settled for me!" Now, we found ourselves praying more, "Lord! Help Us! What do you want for us Lord? That's what we want!"

It's funny, we'd been living together, both believing in the same God and somehow we had been praying selfishly. Each wanting the Lord to give us what we wanted. Now that we'd come back from Grinnel and the experiences we'd gone through there, were beginning to look ahead to what the Lord wanted for us. "What do you want us to do, Lord? Where do you want us to go?"

These were real questions we found ourselves asking. Now, the Lord was where we would direct him. It's exciting to begin to trust the Lord for every detail, not just the major decisions in life!

It's scary too! We wanted to be in control and we knew it. yet, we wanted the Lord to control our lives, our futures. We wanted to do it together.

The last year in seminary was a real training ground for us both for trusting the Lord day by day. This was true as we began to look at the matter of finding a new church home.

Here we are, ex-Catholic and now ex-Lutheran, attending a Presbyterian seminary. "Let's go visit the Assembly of God church this Sunday." I told Sharon. "I'm not ready for that! They're too emotional for me!" She said. We went anyway, and sure enough, they were too emotional.

It was a little church downtown in Dubuque. Only a few families in attendance. We weren't used to their style of worship. Sure, we were open to the Holy Spirit, but when the pastor's wife began wailing and moaning during the service, Sharon whispered to me, "Let's gets out of here, Les. I'm not ready for this stuff!" It would be a long time before Sharon would be comfortable in a Pentecostal church.

We were both raised in the dignity and respect of liturgical worship and even though we were looking for more freedom and power, we were not ready to make such a rapid transaction all at once.

Sharon didn't want to back to that church again. I didn't either! I knew we wouldn't go back. I was out for sure now that I'd been kicked out of the Lutheran church. We talked, during that year in Dubuque about Sharon returning to the Catholic church. At first, it bothered me, but then I could see the Lord was giving me a test. Seeing if I'd be willing to release Sharon and let her return.

"Maybe you should return to the church now." I told Sharon. It had been hard for her. Leaving wasn't easy. She had done it to try to keep peace in the family. Sharon had also been searching for something more than what she had. "I don't understand it, and it doesn't make sense," I said. "But somehow, I feel like maybe you should return."

This lasted about six months during the last year in seminary. I was astounded by the peace that I had over the whole matter. This had to be yet another evidence of the working of the Holy Spirit in our lives.

During this time, we tried many different churches. The pressure from the seminary helped to get us moving. I was disillusioned myself. Not at all sure the Lord wanted us in a church. It seemed as if once we'd come into the charismatic experience, we were free of church structure.

At the same time, however, we found that we would be labeled and put in a box of being Pentecostal, holy rollers and fanatical. I can assure you that we weren't, far from it! We were fast becoming unacceptable for any church. It was all part of the plan that the Lord had for us.

We prayed a lot during those days. Asking only that the Lord would put us somewhere where we could minister for him. We did, however, ask that He put us somewhere that would allow us to stay put for a long time. We were tired of moving now that the kids were getting older, we wanted that. "Maybe some little church near a lake with lots of bass in it, Lord?" had been my prayer. We were hoping for the kids to stay in one school, now that they would soon be entering high school.

The move back from Grinnell the past summer made ten times we'd packed our furniture into the U-Haul and headed down the highway. We were sick of it and our furniture was worn out.

The thoughts of the chaplaincy continued that year until I finally decided I'd better see if there was anything to it. All the time keeping my fingers crossed that it was a mistake and that the Lord had nothing to do with it.

I had been talking one day with the local Army recruiter. He came to school, where I was now counseling part-time in East Dubuque, Illinois. "Have you considered the Army and the Chaplains Corps?" he asked, as we were setting up interviews for the seniors. "The need is great and it's really not that difficult to get in."

"I guess I'd better look into it." I told Sharon one day in the fall of 1973. As soon as I did so, I was surprised to find that one of the key requirements is endorsement from your church.

"Wow, that's something! I don't even have a church, How am I going to get an endorsement?" was my question in prayer. "Come with me! See what I can do!" was the only reply. It should have been enough, but I wasn't satisfied. I had to have more than that!

"...faith is the substance of things hoped for, the evidence of things not seen."[10] I wasn't seeing much those days. I was, however, hoping that the Lord did not want me in the Army.

This continued for several months until about March of 1974. I had finally decided it was time to do something. I had to find out for sure if the Lord was in this or not. All during this time, the devil was roaming around me like a wild boar, trying to tear down our faith and get us to go back to our old ways. He hit me on every side.

"Your transcript has been recalled to Wartburg, for some reason," Herb Manning, registrar at Dubuque Seminary said to me one day. "I don't know what's up, but they got it back and aren't about to let it go. You'd better get over there and see what's up, Les!" he advised.

Reluctantly, I went. I was not crazy about going. I did find out that I had owed $10.00 at the bookstore and they called it back for that reason. I paid the bill, but the transcript was not sent back. It wouldn't be either, for several weeks, and only then, after they at Wartburg would be given assurance from Dubuque that I would not be given the Master of Divinity degree. "They have made it clear to us, "Herb explained, " that unless they receive assurances from us of this, they will not release your transcript. Which of course, means all the work done at Wartburg will be wasted." Herb added, "I'd advise you to go ahead and take the Master of Arts degree and let it go at that, Les. It's not right, but they're calling the shots."[15]

I could feel my blood boiling, once again. I wasn't through at Wartburg yet. I wanted to fight back; to get even. How dare they!

The pressure was getting worse and during those weeks, I found myself getting angry and wanting revenge once again. However, I knew now that I had to love them and forgive them, letting the Lord handle it all.

It was late at night that February in 1974, which I got out of bed and went into the kitchen. The house was quiet and I'd been in a battle all night. I could feel the presence of evil all around me.

---

[10] The Book of Hebrews, Chapter 11, verse 1 KJV.

I was in a state of confusion wondering if I'd missed the Lord after all. It had been just one year ago that I'd experienced the power of the Holy Spirit, back in Grinnell. A lot had happened and now I wondered what was going on.

We had wondered about the house that we were living in since last fall. It had been an old tavern that was converted into three unit apartments. We were on the ground level. The couples above us were into drugs and lived together unmarried. This bothered us.

There was also the night, a few months earlier. Sharon awakened me during the middle of the night, "Les, wake up! Please pray with me! I just feel the presence of evil so strongly!" Erik, our youngest had also been awakened and woke up calling out, "Mommy! Who's in here!"

Reluctantly, we had got up from bed and went through the apartment room by room praying and casting out Satan in the Name of Jesus Christ.

Now, among all of this confusion, I wondered if the Lord had heard our prayer. "I need some answers Lord, show me what's going on anyway, will you?" I asked. "I know you don't want me to fight back and yet it is as if you are asking me to do it. How can this be?"

It would be a long night as I sought to find peace in this confusion. "How can all of this be happening? Men who claim to be your servants doing these things?" I prayed out to God from the bottom of my heart.

"Get into my Word and listen to my voice!" someone seemed to be saying. "The answer is to be found in my Word as I lead you by my Spirit!" At once, I grabbed my Bible and began leafing through it. It was unmistakably the Holy Spirit. "Read Luke, Chapter 7, verses 28-35!"

I wasn't familiar with the passage at all. Quickly, I opened to Luke and read it. It was the Living Bible and did it ever come alive for me that night!

It was Jesus talking about himself and John the Baptist. How all had agreed that God's requirements were right. All that is, except the Pharisees and the teachers of the law. They had rejected God's plan.

Jesus had gone on to compare these men with children and how they reacted to John and his not drinking, calling him crazy. Then, they turned around and called Jesus a drunkard because he drank and associated with sinners.

This was all speaking to me, but I still didn't see the entire scope yet. Then, I read verse 35.

"But I am sure you can always justify your inconsistencies."

As I read and reread the passage, I began to see what the Lord was showing me. I would never be able to figure it all out. There would not be an answer coming. Rather, I'd have to trust in Him.

A wave of Peace came over me as I finally crawled back into bed, being careful not to awaken Sharon. I knew now that the Lord was still in charge of all that was happening. No matter how dark it looked, He'd see us through. It was a great release.

I had discovered something. If you go to the Lord and ask Him to come into your life, as I had done, then ask Him to take over total control of your life, as I had done that night in Grinnell, going to Him at a time of decision or crisis, becomes the natural thing to do. It wasn't easy but it was becoming easier.

It wouldn't be long before we'd be doing more and more every day. Just that past summer, He had shown us how able He is to lead us to the exact place that he wants us! It happened while taking a class in the summer session.

I was to get together to study and to prepare for a project with a Catholic priest in the class. Sharon and I had been starved for some spiritual fellowship and didn't know where to begin to look.

This one evening, I felt a strong leading to go to see the priest. He wasn't expecting me and I didn't have his number. I just went and found his room number. Getting out of the elevator, I found his room and knocked on his door. He answered immediately, "Hi, Les! What are you doing here? I'm just on my way out. I've been invited to go to a prayer meeting. Would you like to go along?" Before I knew it, I said, "Yes, I sure would," and off we went.

It was a Catholic Charismatic meeting, and as it turned out it was just what we were looking for in fellowship. Since it was Catholic, both Sharon and I were a little uncomfortable at first. They loved the Lord, there was no doubt about that. What did bother us, however, was the things we saw after the meeting ended. The language was sometimes bad and many of those present smoked. This was difficult for us to understand.

It didn't seem to fit. It was clearly where the Lord wanted us, we knew that. It wall started because I had obeyed the leading of the Spirit and having gone over to visit the priest seemed rather foolish at the time.

In fact, just a couple of weeks back, I had gone to a meeting alone and was startled when four Catholic sisters approached me afterward. "We feel like the Lord would have us pray for you. Will you come with us now and let us obey the Lord and pray with you?" they asked. I went gladly. A little amused as I thought about what Sharon would think if she knew I was going off with 4 sisters, to say nothing of what my family back in Wisconsin would think. It all seemed so natural.

In fact, I knew it was the Lord as they began to pray and prophesy over me. "The Lord has a special ministry for you of faith and trusting in him, follow after him and listen to Him as He speaks to you through His word. Pick out the promises of My Word. My Word. The promises of My Word? Pick out the promises!" That was the message given to me through the sisters.

They told me to study and read the 40th Chapter of Isaiah. The whole chapter, but especially the last several verses.

"He gives power to the worn out and tired, and strength to the weak…they that wait upon the Lord shall renew their strength."[11]

Yes, I was becoming worn and tired and now He has promised to renew my strength! That really blessed me and encouraged me to press onward, in spite of all that was going on around me.

"Come with me! See What I can do!" That was the promise! The word was full of promises; all that I had to do was to claim them.

This encouraged me to look for a church that would ordain me. I knew now, somehow that the Lord wanted me in a church. Maybe not the Army, at least, I still hoped not. Perhaps he's using this Army stuff just to get me into a church! I thought.

Sharing this with Dr. Bloesch, my friend and advisor now at Dubuque, he suggested, "Why don't you try the United Church of Christ? They need Pastors and really need conservative pastors these days." I wasn't very interested, however. "I'd heard about that church! They even have

---

[11] The Book of Isaiah, Chapter 40, verse 29, NEV.

homosexual ministers and are much too liberal for me!" I told him.

He didn't give up on me, and finally I decided to look into it. They didn't turn me down; in fact, they were very friendly toward me.

If it hadn't been for my not wanting to miss the leading of the Lord, I would have never considered that church. As it turned out, just before the year ended, I met with the care committee to be interviewed.

They interviewed me at length about my beliefs and my plans for ministry, sent me out for deliberations and then called me back. "We have now considered your request to be taken under care and want to inform you that even though we don't believe like you believe, because of our policy of unity in diversity, we now have voted to take you under care as a candidate for the ministry of ordination."

But at least they were up front and honest with me. I liked that, even if they didn't believe the way that I did, they respected my right to believe the way that I wanted.

And so it was, that as the school year drew to an end, in May of 1974, it looked as if the Lord would maybe put me in the Army after all. I now had my paperwork in and was waiting for something to happen.

"A man's mind plans his way, but the Lord directs his steps."[12] I was trying to let the Lord direct my steps. I didn't want the Army. "Maybe that is why He's asking me to go there." I told Sharon one day, as we waited impatiently for something to happen.

"We've come too far to turn back now." Sharon said, as we prayed together that the Lord would reveal his will for us. Yes, the best was yet to come!

I suppose one of the most encouraging things to happen that year had been when I called Marcus Reitz, back in Grinnell. I felt for some time that I should call him, putting it off for fear of his reaction.

"I did get thrown out of Wartburg, Marcus. However, I was accepted at Dubuque seminary and will graduate this May. It's been a pretty rough year, but the Lord is with us and leading us into the Army chaplaincy." I told Marcus.

---

[12] The Book of Proverbs, Chapter 16, verse 9, NKJV.

His response was something I hadn't counted on, but turned out to be a blessing. "Yah, I knew about the meeting. In fact, they called me from the seminary the day that they had the meeting. They tried to get me to do their dirty work, but I refused." He said. " I could see then what they were doing and I refused to go along with them. They wanted me to say that your internship was unsuccessful and I refused to do it." He concluded.

I felt at peace after my conversation with Marcus that day. Like the Lord was somehow bringing us together and showing us both a little more of what He could do if we were willing to just come along with Him.

Led as a Sheep to the Slaughter

Graduation at the seminary was set for the first week of May 1974. It had been a long, hard four years, but now looked like we were finally ready to get to work for the Lord.

We were ready, and now with graduation only weeks away, I still had no job. I had put in the paperwork for the Army chaplaincy, so when I received the call from St. Louis, I wasn't surprised. "Yes, I am ready to go on active duty. I am due to graduate from the seminary in May," I told Chaplain Sullivan. He was calling from the Regional Personnel Center to see if I was available.

"We have everything we need on our end. We have an opening in the basic course coming up in June. However, we are missing one item," he continued, "We need a letter of endorsement from your church. Without that letter, we can't do any more about starting you on active duty."

This was all new to me. I found out some time later that I should not even have applied to the Army without first getting the approval of the church. I had a lot to learn about the differences in policy between the church and the Army. Chaplain Sullivan continued, "As soon as we get the letter from your church, we can get you into school. In fact, all we really need is a phone call from them. I'd advise you to call your head agent and ask them if they will call me. Let's see, you're with the United Church of Christ, aren't you? Call Leon Dickenson in New York and have him give me a call!"

That sounded simple enough to me. Just call Leon Dickenson! I had not met him. I'd only been taken under the care of the church a few months earlier. Now it looks like the only thing preventing my going into the Army was that phone call.

But I still wasn't ready to go into the Army and was still hoping that I wouldn't have to. I knew that I would have to go through with this. By this time, graduation was just a few days off. I'd already given notice to our landlord that we'd be leaving the apartment. This meant, we'd have to get out soon.

Where do we go? We wound wonder as we waited for something to happen. The Army recruiter, who lived up the street from us, and helped get the paperwork squared away, offered the use of his garage to store our furniture, if we needed it.

I could see that we were to need somewhere to go after finally getting a hold of Reverend Leon Dickenson. "I'm calling about the endorsement to the Army chaplaincy," I said. "They are ready to take me on active duty, and need to hear from you." I could tell he wasn't to wild about hearing from me. This wasn't the way that he was used to doing business.

"There should have been a meeting with our office before you went ahead and applied to the Army," he informed me. "This could be a real problem! We are way over our quota's in the Army and since you are neither black nor female, it doesn't look like we'll be able to help you."

"What's this? Black? Female?" I thought. "It sounded like reverse discrimination!"

We talked further and he concluded our conversation by reiterating, "Yes, if you were black or a female, we could help you out real quick, but since you're neither, it doesn't look like we can do much for you!"

It was a shocker for me. "How could this guy just come right out and say a thing like that? First, they told me, we don't believe what you believe, but we'll ordain you anyway! Now this! What kind of a church is this?" I wondered.

There were more dark days ahead as we waited for something to happen. It was by faith that we gave up our apartment and moved our furniture into storage. There was no way that we would get into the Army by June.

Somehow, I had a feeling still that the Lord wanted us in the Army. That's all I had. The Iowa District of the United Church had been after me to take a church in central Iowa. I assured them that I would be going into the Army and wouldn't be available for a call.

Somebody was trying to tell me something. "How about this Lord? I was sure that you wanted me in the Army and now this?" Since I had now burned all of my bridges behind me and the door appeared to be closed for the Army, I agreed to come out and talk with them about the church call.

"Okay, I'll come out and talk with you, but understand that the Lord is calling me into the chaplaincy and even if I did accept the job, it's likely I wouldn't be there very long." I informed them.

"Oh yes, we understand. We'll plan on seeing you on the fifteenth of June, then." They had hired me as their pastor.

That gave us just enough time to drive back to Wisconsin and visit family and friends before going out to Iowa for the meeting with the church. I had an offer of a good job with the county as an alcohol and drug counselor through the court services. The pay was good and it was a job that seemed like something I would enjoy.

However, I had a sense that if I took that job, the door to the chaplaincy would be permanently closed. I didn't feel right about that. Sure, it would have been a great way out, and then I wouldn't have to worry about going in the service for sure. More than that, I didn't want to miss the direction of the Lord. I'd done too much of that already.

If I went to Iowa, the door would still be open. Just a crack, at best, but still open. Off we went to Blairsburg! The Lord's timing is always perfect! Never too early, never too late! He was showing us his way of waiting up to the last minute to come through. Had we moved out of the house a day earlier, we'd have missed the telephone call. Since we had no mailbox, the church would not have been able to contact us!

Entering Blairsburg, the sign on the road read "population 300". I often wondered where they all were, since over the next two years, I hardly saw more than forty in attendance on Sunday mornings. It certainly wasn't my ideal place to be doing the Lord's work. Besides, I knew that just maybe, that's why the Lord led me there! He knew it just as well as He knew me!

We hit the ground running after the interview and the trial sermon, which I passed with flying colors, despite the fact that I gave that sermon in my tennis shoes. We were virtually living out of the tent and camping at this point and all of the rest of our clothes were packed away back in Dubuque, ready for the next step.

Dubuque is home to many slaughterhouses as well as seminaries. Cattle, sheep and hogs are trucked in from all parts of the state for butchering. Slaughter used in the informal sense can mean a thorough defeat; or to defeat thoroughly or to trounce. I felt as though that summed up my personal experiences in Dubuque the past few years.

Leaving all of that behind, I was certain that all of the defeat was behind me too. They didn't have a slaughterhouse in Blairsburg, yet another thorough defeat awaited me. One, which was required in my learning, to be led by the Spirit.

Now that I was a sheep, I had to learn to let the Shepherd lead. Sheep are sheared on a routine basis, and do so without making a sound. Sometimes the sheep are slaughtered. The thought of either had kept me from getting too close to the Shepherd for a long time. Now that I'd started to get closer to him, I'd been learning some lessons I should have learned years earlier.

It was nice and quiet in Blairsburg. Not much going on except in spring and fall. First crops are planted and then harvested. "Don't be surprised, pastor, if you don't see me in church the next several weeks! I haven't forgotten about the church, it's just that I gotta get the crop in when she's ready. You'll understand, won't you?" I was informed by several of my congregation that first fall. Sure enough, they meant it. Attendance dropped significantly during the time for beans and corn to be harvested.

But, since attendance wasn't all that great before, the drop was noticeable. I was comforted to know that at least it wasn't my preaching that was keeping them away. I had always been concerned about that ever since the day my uncle, Carl Simonson, shook my hand after hearing me preach that first sermon back at the home church in Mt. Morris. "It was a good sermon, Leslie, only problem was that it was too long." I had never forgotten that and hoped that I wasn't driving them away.

I really tried to seek the Lord for his message. I knew where I was and wanted to see the people get on fire for the Lord badly. Because of this, I found myself spending much at the altar in prayer about the message. The only time I saw my flock was on Sunday morning and then only about one-third or less showed up. I wondered about the other two-thirds and how I could reach them.

I've always been bad at remembering names, I was embarrassed when I'd meet one of the faithful on the streets of Webster City. "Hello, pastor! How are you today?" I would meet them after church as they left very quickly and introduced themselves. I felt as though I should remember their names. I was expected to know them, and I'm sure they were disappointed when I didn't remember their name.

They were patient and understanding, and would give me time to get adjusted. "After all, our pastor is young and just out of seminary," would be a common phrase around town.

As I continued to seek the Lord for direction, it seemed like I got only one message time and time again. "Tell my people, and all of those who are seeking after Me, that I have shown my love for them all in my son, Jesus Christ."

It seemed too simple! After all, most of these folks were raised in the church. Surely they had heard that message all of their lives! I wanted to tell them about walking in the Spirit and being filled with the Spirit. That is what I wanted to share with them.

The Lord had other plans, "Preach only about Jesus Christ and the power He has to restore those who come to him into the right relationship with Me!"

I obeyed the best that I could. The Spirit assured me time and time again, "If the people will step forth to receive Him, they will at the same time receive great joy." That seemed to make sense and after all, wasn't that what we all wanted. "I surely couldn't go wrong with that message, could I?"

Yes, the Lord has assured me, during those times of prayer, "If they will come unto Me, they will receive the glorious salvation of their souls."

As I continued to preach the very simple message of Jesus and His love, I began to see and feel resistance. Resistance is something that I had never dealt with easily. It meant personal rejection and that hurt me deeply. It was a sign of defeat for me. A real trouncing was in the making.

So, once again, I sought the Lord. "Yours is to be a ministry of trusting and obeying me!" He assured me time and time again. "What you do for me, you need not be ashamed of, and if you will go forth in boldness proclaiming my son, Jesus Christ, and Him crucified, I will take care of the rest." I knew he could do it, but it was still rough as the attendance began to drop, even after the harvest season had long passed. "Could it be that my preaching is driving them away?" I wondered, "Maybe, just maybe, Uncle Carl was right after all," I told Sharon one day. "The kids have been hearing things at school," she said. "They don't know what to make of it. What do you think I should tell them, Les?"

I was sure that the Lord had opened the door for us to come to Blairsburg, but I was beginning to doubt some now. "How can you be in this Lord? What about the Chaplaincy? I was sure you wanted us in it."

I had faith but I was getting weak. Deep down I still felt that He did want us in the Army, but as time went on, it seemed like it would become more and more impossible. He had opened the door for this, surely He could open the door for that as well.

It was a cold January night in 1975 when the Lord confirmed his presence with us in a rather unusual way. It was way below zero that morning and I had arrived at the church early to prepare for the Sunday service. "We had a break in last night, here at the church!" Mrs. Prusmann, our janitor, announced frantically. "They almost knocked me over as they were leaving this morning! I don't know how they would have gotten in! I am sure that I had locked the door before leaving last night! I never leave it open." She was hysterical as she tried to make sense of what had happened. "Nothing seems to be missing, but wait until the deacons hear about this!"

As I tried to calm her, I walked into my office and saw a $1.00 bill on my desk, with a note attached to it, it read:

Thank you for the place to stay last night

No man can open the door unless God permit and no man can close the door unless God permit.

Signed,

The Traveling Trio, Brothers Judd, Bill and Brian

I knew that this was a special message from the Lord for me. I needed to know that and He sent those boys to tell me in a special way. He was still in charge. My faith soared!

News travels fast in Blairsburg and it wasn't long before the whole town knew what had happened. In fact, before the day ended, a new lock was put on the front door of the church. The fact that it was Sunday and no one worked on Sunday seemed to make little difference.

Yes, the Lord would open a new door, whatever that door was, in His own time. I had wished He'd hurry up, but sheep aren't to talk back. They follow the Shepherd, even if it means being sheared or facing slaughter. Lead me Lord!

We did see a few respond to the message of Christ. Others seemed to be drawing back in frustration, not really knowing what to do. The Holy Spirit was doing his work, convicting of sin, of judgment and of righteousness.

"How about riding along with me to Webster City, Les?" Dr. Marv Boyer said one cold winter day as he stopped by the office. I'd not had this happen before and I thought it rather strange. Dr. Boyer was one of my deacons and also the Superintendent of Schools. A very influential man in town and in the church.

"Sure, I'd be glad to ride along," I said. All was fine until we stopped at the church on the return trip. He caught me off guard when he said, "I know it's tough getting started in a new position and not having had any experience, maybe I can give you a little advice. There are many people in the church who are concerned about the drop in attendance," he stated. "This drop in attendance means less money coming in. I want to be of help to you in any way I can," Marvin assured me. "There is also a lot of talk going on around town about your preaching. Maybe you could consider changing your style, or something," was his very sincere suggestion.

I began to feel myself bristle as he was telling me how to do my job. "I'd never consider coming over to the school and telling him how to do his job, Who does he think he is, anyway?"

I could feel my face flush as he continued, "Some people are wondering why you always ask people to come forward? Is it because you want them to admit that they're sinners or something?" he asked.

As if that wasn't enough, before I could respond, he dropped another bomb on me. "I need to tell you that many of the folks in church are unhappy that you're not visiting them more often."

That did it! "I happen to feel that it's more important for me to spend my time visiting the sick and shut-in and those who are not attending church!" I blurted very defensively.

That was only the beginning. At least now it was out in the open. I had known something was not right and now it was confirmed. It didn't make it any less painful, however. The old feeling of rejection and failure began to surface once again.

I felt like quitting right then and there. "I don't need this kind of job." I muttered to Sharon. She had to get all the frustration. I knew that wasn't the answer. I had to trust the Lord to open and close the doors. I didn't like it, but that's the way it had to be.

As much as I hated the thought of ever going into the Army, it now began to look pretty good. From where I was, anything would be an improvement.

The door wasn't completely closed, but it didn't look good. The United Church said the best they could do would be to endorse me for a reserve chaplaincy. "If that doesn't work, then I'll know for sure that the Lord doesn't want me in," I thought as I began checking into it.

It didn't take long to find the prospects bleak. "All the more chance for the Lord to do something." I told Sharon, as I plowed ahead. Sure enough, out of the blue, a slot opened up and I soon had a job as a Chaplain of an Army Reserve unit down in Des Moines.

This news didn't go over well at the church, as I began to hear rumblings about the pastor being gone to Reserve meetings all the time. It was hard for them to share their pastor with anyone. You couldn't blame them for that. After all, they were paying me. I made $333.00 every two weeks. The monthly salary, $666.00, a number of no little significance for some.

I thought nothing of it at the time, however, as the years passed, it became a family joke among the boys. They thought it was rather funny. I guess maybe it was, and still is.

What we were going through was no laughing matter, however. I'd been there less than a year and it was beginning to look like I wouldn't be able to stay much longer if something didn't happen soon.

It broke loose at the annual meeting of the congregation. "We are running into a financial crisis, if we don't get some more money coming in soon, We'll be in big trouble!" The treasurer announced.

I knew that I was being held directly responsible since the money came from the offerings. Almost all the money came from a very few of the congregation, and if they stopped giving it would be curtains. Since over half of all offerings went to pay my salary, it didn't take long for me to figure out what was going on.

Soon after that, the money that they had been paying me for travel expenses came into question. That really made me mad. "Now they're questioning my integrity!" I told Sharon after the emergency financial meeting that evening.

I, long ago, had been sheared and now it seemed that slaughter was imminent. It looked like a thorough defeat. Just what I need, I guess, but certainly not what I wanted.

I had to admit, it was easier than it had been in the past now that I had experienced the power of the Holy Spirit, but still not without pain.

Yes, I could relate to the passage from Isaiah 53:

"He was led as a sheep to slaughter, and as a lamb is silent before the shearers, so he opened not his mouth; in his humiliation, justice was denied him; and who can express the wickedness of the people of his generation?"[13]

I was being humiliated, justice was being denied me and on top of that, I had to remain silent. Believe me, I sought the Lord, and I sought him diligently! Each time I got the same message, *"Yours is to be a min-*

---

[13] The Book of Isaiah, Chapter 53, Verses 7-9, NIV.

istry of trusting and obeying Me! If you will go forth in boldness proclaiming my Son, Jesus Christ and Him crucified, I will take care of the rest."

"Okay, Lord, I'm trying but it's getting tough." I prayed many times that year.

In late February 1975, the Lord answered our prayer in a most powerful and unusual way. We found ourselves within a Charismatic meeting at the Dow United Methodist Church. It was cold outside, but warm inside as Reverend Leland Davis, teacher and prophet, from Tempi, Arizona ministered on the gift of personal prophecy.

But this was all new to Sharon and me, even though we had been walking in the Spirit for over two years now. We had never seen such a move of the Holy Spirit as we saw Rev. Davis speak the prophetic word to individual members of the body.

If ever anyone needed a word from God, it was us! So, we returned on the second night, we came expecting! We had been introduced to him on the night before, but he knew absolutely nothing of our situation.

We were so excited to hear Rev. Davis call us up to the front, and even more excited as we heard what he was telling up in the Spirit. It hit our situation exactly. There was no possible way he could have known what we were going through at the time. I was certain it was the Lord! The message built our faith and sent us on our way, rejoicing! His message was this:

I see the acceleration of God's promises in your lives. I see the Holy Spirit moving and melting resistance. There are some at the moment who feel like they are opposed to you or at odds with you and what God is doing. You are going to see God's victory and triumph in their lives. I see minds that are conditioned by traditions and associations from intellectual forces. God is going to melt that intellectualism in the lives of others, as He worked in you as a prophetical manifestation in your own life.

He is going to begin to work in the lives of some that feel as though they know all the answers but in their hearts, hunger for reality, and through the word of thy tongue, the word that destroys the yoke, and the liberation of thy speech in the life of faith. There shall be a propagation in the hearts of those that hear thee a hunger, appetite and desire, and the Lord shall not disappoint nor shall he turn away empty. Your hands shall be full as the dispenser of the bread of life. The Lord shall use thee and feed the hunger of many spirits.

Gladness shall spring forth and the song of the Lord shall produce, shall sing in thine heart, son. Even if oppression shall arise and sudden opposition, the Lord shall be thy defender and He shall build about thee the hedge of his name to protect thee from the unsought of thine enemy and you shall know that the Lord reign.

He is victor, and you shall walk without fear even in the midst of those that at the time are thine enemies. As thy always pleases the Lord, He shall make even thine enemies to be at peace with thee.[14]

It was still cold outside that night as we drove back to Blairsburg, but our hearts had been strongly warmed by the Spirit if the living God. This message carried us through some rough times. We just knew that if we walked in ways that were pleasing to the Lord, He would take care of the rest.

The prophecy had been further confirmed later that day while visiting one of my most faithful farm families. In fact, the Osies had given us a pie the past winter to help feed our family. "I just don't understand what's going on," Mrs. Osey said, "We've been members of this church for almost 25 years now. We've heard just about everything preached. All you have been preaching to us is Jesus Christ, and the people are more fired up than they've ever been before. I just don't understand it."

It is sometimes hard to understand, but that's exactly what happened. In fact, it seems to happen whenever and wherever Christ is preached, even in the best of churches.

I just knew now it was time to make preparations to leave Blairsburg. I was not at all sure how that would come about, but I knew that our time there was getting short.

"How do you stand on the choice for the new material for the Sunday school pastor?" Peggy Stafford asked. I had tried to stay out of the issue, but now I had to take astand. "I favor the Cook material over the official United Church material." I said. Peggy was a faithful member of the con-

---

[14] Personal Prophecy by Reverend Leland Davis, Dows, IA, February 1975.

gregation and very active in District and State church organizations. Cam, her husband, was a member of the State board. They were dedicated folks and it hurt me to have to take a stand against them.

But I knew that I had no other choice. It was then that I applied through my reserve unit for the basic course for Chaplain training. "The course is nine weeks ling, Chaplain." The Pac NCO informed me. "We have had no schools approved this year because of the money shortage. You'll never get it! Your chances are about 1 in 100,000, but I'll go ahead and put it through."

I thanked him and said a prayer. "Okay, Lord, just another chance for you to work. If you don't open it for me, I'll know at least you don't want me in the Army."

I had to get this thing with the Army Chaplaincy settled. It had gone on too long now, but I couldn't shake the feeling that that's where I was supposed to be.

Very reluctantly, then, I began to investigate the possibilities of a transfer to the Assemblies of God. I say very reluctantly, because both Sharon and I had agreed that was the church we didn't want. Now that it was sure the United Church of Christ would not put me on active duty, it meant I'd have to have another church if I was going on active duty.

"Guess what," I told Sharon after reading the requirements for ordination. "In order to be an Assemblies pastor, I have to be baptized by immersion! That's the only thing I don't have yet." Her response surprised me, "Oh, that's not so bad. I'd been thinking we ought to both be baptized that way. That's the way they did it in the early church, and I think we should do it, even if you don't go with the Assemblies."

We believed in baptism and had both been baptized as babies. So had all of our children been baptized. Three as Catholics and one as a Lutheran. I resisted mainly because I felt baptism wasn't required for salvation anyway, according to the scripture.

"Will you baptize me and my wife and 2 of our children?" I asked Rev. Clay Noah of the First Baptist Church in Webster City, soon after that. He thought I wanted to use his church to perform a baptism at first, since we had none at ours. When he finally got the message, he was a little shocked and surprised.

But then so were a lot of our congregation back in Blairsburg. "I don't understand why they want to baptized again. Isn't infant baptism good enough?" they asked. We invited the whole congregation to attend the Sunday evening services. However, only a few couples showed up.

It was then that we decided we needed to put out a fleece before the Lord to find out where he wanted us next. I didn't feel much like Gideon, but maybe I was, in a way. He wasn't too anxious to go up against those Midianites, nor was I anxious to go back to the Army. I had to find out.

Something Resembling a Fleece

It was in the worst time of his life that the Angel of the Lord appeared to Gideon and said, *"Mighty soldier, the LORD is with you!"* Gideon wasted no time in responding. *"If the Lord is with us, why has all of this happened to us?"*[15]

This wasn't exactly the worst time in my life. I guess I'd been through worse, but I was wondering where the Lord was. I knew the Lord was with me and promised to give me the strength to do all things.

What we ahd been through the past couple of years had strengthened our faith and trust in Him. This thing bout the Army was really getting to me, however.

"Why hadn't the Lord just gone ahead and put me back there in Dubuque when I thought for sure He was going to?" That still bothered me. *"A man's mind plans his way, but the LORD directs his steps!"*[16] That was clearly part of it, and I knew it! As much as I tried to get it out of my mind, I knew that I had to trust the Lord.

I'd blown it so many times in the past that I didn't want that to happen again. Doing my own thing and leaving the Lord out! That was not what I

---

[15] The Book of Judges, Chapter 6, verse 13, The Living Bible.

[16] The book of Proverbs, Chapter 16, verse 9, NIV.

wanted. Looking at the big metal cross around my neck, I remembered what Jane, my sister-in-law, said to me back in November of 1974. It was my ordination day and as she handed the cross to me, she said, "This is a special gift from God, Les. I gave your name to a guy up in Northern Wisconsin. He makes these crosses, but only puts the message out that the Lord gives him after praying about it for a long time." She said. I looked at the cross and saw the simple message, "THY WILL BE DONE." It spoke to me, and at once, I knew that it had to be from the Lord.

But it had been a long time getting to the place where I could be honest and pray, "Not my will, but your will, Lord. That's what I want."

So, I suppose, the fleece was as much a desire to find out what the Lord wanted me to do, as it was the desire to make sure I didn't end up doing what I wanted.

I was about to learn an important lesson, it's a lot easier to pray strong prayers and even fleeces, or something resembling a fleece, if you don't want to do something than if you do want to do something.

If I had wanted badly to go into the Army, I'm sure now I'd never have prayed the way I did. In fact, I'm sure that's why Gideon prayed his fleece.[17] He put the Lord to the test and asked him to prove to him that He did, in fact, want him to go into battle.

I was about to put the Lord to the test and ask Him to prove to me that He did want me in the Army. The test began soon after I got the call from Chaplain Gorden Hanson, reserve chaplain for my area. "We just got the word on your request for extended active duty to attend the Chaplain Basic Course, Les. It's been approved, and you are to report to Fort Wadsworth, New York on 4 January, 1976." He informed me excitedly. "This is very surprising to me Les, since we haven't been able to get these through before!"

Gordie had seemed to take a special interest in my family and me ever since we'd first met. This surprised me since he was a Lutheran of the same synod I'd been with. "Let me know if there's anything that I can do for you. The orders should be coming to you. If they don't get to you before the end of the year, go ahead out there without them." He said.

---

[17] The Book of Judges, Chapter 6, verse 36-40, NIV.

So it was then that I laid out the first part of the fleece before the Lord. Sharon and I were in this together now and we prayed, "Lord, we are going to resign as pastor here at Blairsburg, effective December 31st 1975." It was now late September, which would give the congregation about 90 days notice, with plenty of time to find a replacement.

"We are asking that you prove this to us by getting us an endorsement from a church." The one that I had received from the United Church of Christ was only good for reserve duty, but it would get us into school.

It looked like the Assemblies of God was the best bet at the time, but there were a lot of things that looked bad from their point of view.

They hardly knew me, I was in a very liberal church, had never served in one of their churches, I had no roots there, nor did I have any connections. No connection that is, except the Lord.

I did, at the time write to the Assemblies and start the paperwork required. I knew I would have to get an endorsement somehow before going active.

I guess, at that point, I had one up on Gideon. Before the first fleece was answered, I laid out another one. Since I didn't want to go, I had nothing to lose and everything to gain.

It is my understanding that the purpose of the fleece is to ask the Lord to do something that would otherwise be impossible and could not happen in the natural course of events. Okay, Lord, now if and when you get us this endorsement, Sharon and I prayed, "We need to know for sure that we will be going from the school right into active duty and we have to know it before we graduate from school!"

Little did we know, as we prayed, what we were asking. Before it was over, there would be many people thinking we were crazy and outright brazen. We never told anyone else about our fleece until it was over.

As I arrived at the school in New York, leaving Sharon and the kids back in the Iowa parsonage, I felt led of the Spirit to write a letter to Dr. Gannon, Chairman of the Commission on Chaplains with the Assemblies of God.

I knew from correspondence with him that the next meeting of the Commission was July 1976, at which time I'd be expected to meet with them for consideration. They had to meet me. Plus the meeting, I knew that they had a hard and fast requirement that anyone being endorsed serve a minimum of 2 years in an Assemblies church before being endorsed.

I had to make the request to have a special meeting and also waiver of the church requirement if the Lord was going to answer that fleece. It was a bold request. One I'd just as soon not have made, but it had to be done. I got no peace until I wrote that letter and once I did, peace came.

It was cold in New York in January 1976, and I could hardly believe I was back in the Army, if even for only nine weeks. Which I was sure, it would be. We lived in the BBQ at Fort Hamilton and crossed the double-decked bridge connecting Brooklyn and Staten Island.

Fort Hamilton and Fort Wadsworth had been built many years earlier to help defend the harbor from enemy attacks. Now we were there to learn how to be officers and chaplains. It soon brought back a lot of unpleasant memories. Memories I had tried to forget but couldn't.

The uniform was one of them. We wore it every day to classes. Did PT every day also. "I can take whatever they want to throw at me," I thought, "I'll only be here 9 weeks anyway, and then somewhere else. I'm sure the Lord doesn't want me in the Army! Where does he want me? I have no idea, but we'll cross that bridge when we come to it."

It was a month after I'd written the letter before a reply came. It began, "My dear Brother Simonson, that was the first time I'd been called a brother, in a letter, that wasn't the Lutheran way, nor was it the UCC way! He began, "I've taken the time to share your letter with another member of the Commission on Chaplains, and also to discuss this matter with one of the officers in the Chief's office. The appeal that you have made to this office is the most difficult one to respond to."

I could see it didn't look good from the start. In fact, it got worse as it went along. They were sure I was trying to force them. Rev. Gannon said, "We have a firm conviction that God knows all of these things ahead of time and He is well able to demonstrate His ability to move on our behalf without undue pressure and without trying to force the issue into untimely deadlines."

It didn't take long for me to get the message. They were not at all happy with my letter. All I could do was to give it to the Lord and trust Him with it. I had taken my stand and now I had to wait.

If I'd been discouraged before, it helped little to read further:

"...Even if we were to call a special meeting of the commission on chaplains, I could not guarantee that if granted ecclesiastical endorsement you would be the next person that would receive selection by the Commission for active duty. We are over quota in all branches of the service, and at the same time have a backlog of individuals having previously received endorsement..."

There was little doubt now that the Lord would have to do something or there was no way I could ever get into the Army. In a way, I felt good about that, and yet in a way, I didn't. I had faith the Lord could do it, but would he? I'd have to wait and see. I still have almost a month left in school and can't be sure until that time.

Yes, I was a little discouraged by the letter, as Rev. Gannon had suggested, as he closed his long letter. I guess you'd say I had mixed feelings since I was kind of encouraged and discouraged one and the same time. "Without doubt," Rev. Gannon finished his letter, "this letter will be a little disappointing to you, Brother Simonson, but remember, He orders our footsteps...If indeed this is the will of God for your life, let us believe together that this can materialize within the regular order of things..."

At least we were in agreement on one thing; He orders our footsteps! It didn't look like to me it was the will of God for my life to enter the Army Chaplaincy.

Did I get a wild idea soon after that while sitting in class one day. It was a boring class anyway, since I knew I would not likely be using any of this stuff. "Why don't you call the Chief's office and ask if they have any other churches who are looking for chaplains! Man! That's crazy! But then again, what had I got to lose? If I don't call, maybe I'll miss the Lord! Maybe he does have a church in such a position!"

I couldn't shake the idea. Maybe I'm not trusting the Lord if I do that, was my thought. Then again, wasn't Chaplain Dewey Jernigan, Assemblies of God Chaplain working there in that office? What would he think? What would he tell the commission? It would be curtains as far as the Assemblies went. But then, it looked like it was already, so it didn't really matter, did it?

So, working up the courage, one day I decided to help the Lord along a little. Ringing the Chief's office, guess who answers the phone. Right! Dewey himself. "I have just received a letter from Rev. Gannon," I began, "It doesn't look like I'll be going in the Army with the Assemblies. Do you have any other churches that are looking for Chaplains to represent them?" He said nothing, but I could feel the red flags going up!

Where is this guy coming from? Who does he think he is? The fact that I assured him of the strong feeling I had that the Lord wanted me on active seemed to make little difference. I knew he thought I was crazy and way out of line. I should have been more concerned than I was. For some reason, I had a peace about the whole thing.

Two fleeces before the Lord at once; I still didn't have the endorsement and prospects looked bleak. However, I still had time! School wasn't out for a few weeks yet and nothing could be sure until then.

But I had to keep my end of the bargain. The Lord still had time to prove it to me, since I had asked Him to let this happen before I graduated.

The old devil was too busy also. He brought some temptations in the form of job opportunities that I hadn't asked for. I called Sharon back in Iowa that week, and my good friend Berl VinChattle, a farmer and preacher, happened to be there at the time. I told him what was going on and he said to me, "I think maybe your not to go in the Army, Les. In fact, I never thought that you were supposed to go. I have a church in Kansas who's looking for a pastor. How about looking into that? I can give them your name if you'd like."

It was tempting, but I knew I couldn't do it, at least not until March. "Thanks Berl, but I don't think that I can now. Maybe later." I said.

Another temptation came my way on Monday morning, three weeks before graduation. "I spoke to my Bishop over the weekend about your situation, Les," Joe Webb, A United Methodist and National Guard Chaplain from Milwaukee said, "he told me to tell you that if you wanted a church to give him a call right away!" Joe even gave me his phone number.

Boy, was I tempted to make that call right about then. I knew, however, that I could not do anything yet! I'd have to wait, at least until school was out before doing anything. I remember keeping that number, just in case.

Looking back on those situations, I now believe the Lord allowed them to come up so that He could test me a bit. I guess he thought it fair since I was testing Him.

I guess He wanted to see if I would wait or not. I waited, but not without some anxiety.

It was just a regular day, like all the others had been the past 7 weeks. Get on the bus at 6; take a long ride across the bridge from Ft. Hamilton to Ft. Wadsworth; then morning Physical Training; and a cold shower, of course. The Army doesn't know what hot water is. Then it was on to a full day of boring classes in map reading or military tactics and first aid.

"Simonson, report to the front office, you have a phone call!" I hopped up at once wondering who would be calling me. I was hoping that all was well at home.

I was in for a surprise. "Hi, Les, this is Gordie Hanson. How's it going there?" I wasted little time in telling him exactly how things were going. And it seemed strange, him calling me. Sure he's a Chaplain, but Lutheran too! Lutherans stick together, and I had been about as popular with them as ants on a picnic since leaving Wartburg. Most stayed far away. We talked for a while that morning. I told him everything, including my conversation with Dewey. Then I recalled that Gordie knew him well. They had worked together along the way. "Wow! That's neat. Maybe the Lord had something to do with this call." I thought.

As we finished, Gordie said, "Les, is there anything that I can do for you?" I said quickly, "Yes, Gordie, how about calling Dewey and telling him that I'm not crazy! I'm sure that he thinks I am, by now!" "No problem, Les, I'll give him a call today." He said. I went back to class thinking to myself, at least someone understands what I'm going through.

Now the Lord was ready to show me something big. I received a letter from Dr. Gannon. I did not expect this one and wondered what now? Unlike the first, ten days earlier, this one was short and sweet:

> "Dear Brother Simonson, Greetings in Jesus' name! There is a possibility that we will be inviting you to Washington, D.C. at which time you will meet a great number of the members of the Commission on Chaplains and be processed for ecclesiastical endorsement. I will let you know within a few days..."

There it was, right before my eyes. An answer to my fleece! "What's next Lord?"

And sure enough, as he'd written, in a few days the call came. "We want you to come to Washington next Thursday to meet the Commission." He said. "We'll expect you at 2:00pm in Room 376 of the Americana Hotel. Can you make it?"

"Can I make it? Boy, can I! I'll be there!" It didn't take long for me to start praising the Lord! He was passing the test, no doubt about it.

Over the next few days, the hours were filled with excitement! I had trouble containing my thrilled feeling. True, I still had neither the endorsement nor the assurance I'd be going active duty directly from school. Yet, somehow that didn't seem to matter. I knew, I just knew the Lord had heard our fleece. I guess, up until then, I doubted. Now it was real, Halleluiah!

I got a little to excited around school, I'm afraid. Started telling people what was happening. This wasn't exactly the sort of thing that those old Chaplains were used to hearing. Many of them had themselves joined the military to escape the call of the ministry. Like hiding from God and doing it in the name of religion. Something like I'd seen a few years back at the seminary.

It didn't matter now, nothing mattered. The Lord was real and I knew it! I wanted to shout it from the rooftops!

I caught an Amtrak train the following week from Ft. Dix, where we were completing our final week of training. Even on the train, I couldn't contain myself. I began to witness to the other passengers and had received a letter months later from a woman thanking me for the witness. She'd been seeking the baptism of the Holy Spirit and soon after that, received. Praise the Lord!

Arriving at Washington train station, in plain view of our nation's capitol, I became even more thrilled. I called my cousin, John. He worked for HUD in D.C. and was on leave from his teaching job back at the University of Wisconsin at Platteville. "Come on down and pick me up at the train station!" I said. It's not every day that one has the privilege to be driven around Washington D.C. by a PhD., I thought as I waited for him.

He picked me up and drove me to the Americana Hotel. I arrived just in time to make the meeting. I'd wondered if we'd make it with John's old clunker. "You can't afford a better car than this? With all of the money that you're making?" I laughed.

And I called up Dr. Gannon in his room. "Got a problem, Les! Something has come up over at the pentagon, some important briefing. Dewey can't get away." He informed me with some concern. "Come on up anyway, we're going to proceed without him."

Stunned and surprised, I left John, telling him to pick me up in a couple of hours, and headed up. And sure enough, everything was great. No problems and before long, I was asked to leave so that the board could make a decision.

It was a few minutes later they called me in making the news known to me. "We have voted and decided to grant you the endorsement and approval for active duty, pending, of course, the approval of the absent members of the Commission."

I was in the clouds! More than I could stand, once again. Half the fleece was incomplete.

Getting up to leave, I shook Dr. Gannon's hand and said, "I'm sorry Dewey Jerrnigan couldn't make it. I would have liked to meet him, since he's the only one from the Army on the board." No sooner had I spoken these words, than who should appear, so lively and quick! None other than Dewey, an hour and a half late for the meeting. Strange coincidence, maybe. Maybe not!

You see, Dewey had to meet me for the fleece to work. He was in the Chief's office and could influence the second condition.

For obvious reasons, the Lord didn't want him in the first meeting. He'd been against the whole thing; I'm sure, ever since talking to me over the phone earlier. "Didn't want any guy like that representing his church."

Dewey brushed past me and right to Dr. Gannon. "Let's get together and hear what you've decided," he urged. "I'd like to talk to you later. Wait down in the lobby." Was his order.

That's just what I did. It was full of people and I grabbed the first seat available. Striking up a conversation with a woman next to me, I soon discovered it was Dewey's wife.

Another coincidence! Maybe! We talked and soon Dewey walked up, looked at her and then me and then scratching his head "Did you two meet?"

He had a lot of questions for me. "What would you have done had the Commission not accepted you? Would you seek out another church to endorse you?" He was anxious and stirred up, I could tell. I saw what the Lord had in mind by keeping him away.

"Since you now have a job, what about your family? How will you live? Where will you go?" were some of his questions. I had no answers, none at least that he would want to hear. I had the feeling like maybe; he'd been in the Army too long himself. I guess that's why I said, "You should understand, Dewey. The Lord will provide for us."

"Yeah, sure, I know that, but what will you do? Where will you live?" he went on, "There's nothing open with the Army until after July. You understand that, don't you? Everything is full."

I said a silent Praise the Lord to myself as we talked. "All the more chance for you to work." Dewey continued, "I'm concerned about you and your family. Maybe I can let you know how it looks for July when I get back to the office."

And I said nothing. Knowing that wouldn't be good enough. I had to know I'd be going active right after graduation or else. July wasn't gonna cut it. "I should be able to let you know something before you leave school," he said, as John arrived to pick me up and we parted.

"What do you want to see first, Les? The capitol building or the Watergate?" John asked as we drove towards downtown. "We don't hve much time to see the town, but let's get in what we can. How long can you stay?" he asked. "I have to start back tomorrow, so we better make it fast."

And sure enough, we saw plenty that night.

John and I had grown up together back in Wisconsin and now that the years had slipped by, it was a special time.

Washington was a rather unlikely place for us to get together, however. Our folks back home would only dream about being in a place like this. They never hardly had the chance to leave the state.

"Is that Barry Goldwater, down on the floor?" I asked, as we entered the Senate that day. And sure enough, it was. I had always been thrilled by his manner, and now I'd actually see him in action.

And then, stopping by on the house side, we stopped by Congressman Steigers office. Just imagine he was in! "It is great to see you here." He said. "I just wish Sharon and the kids could see all of this!" I told John as we left the capitol and headed for the White House.

"It's rough around here after dark, Les. This is a high crime area." I found that hard to grasp. All the impressive buildings and the great history of our country surrounded by crime and lawlessness! I didn't want to believe it, but I knew that John would give it to me straight.

We went across town toward the monuments. It was now getting dark and the lights were on. It was a beautiful sight to behold. I didn't want to leave and caught myself forgetting why I had come to town. I would soon be back in Chaplain's training. A few more days and it would be all finished. I told John that night as we ate some of that fine Washington Seafood, "it's a pretty exciting life you're leading." John confided, "Sometimes I think that I should have stayed in the Army."

And after assuring him that he had made the right choice, we talked late into the night in his little, D.C. apartment. I got back to Ft. Dix just in time to pack up and head back to Ft. Wadsworth and the final week of school. And now I waited, as excited as a little kid waiting for Santa to come. I just knew it would happen and couldn't wait.

Sure enough, it did! Not at all like I'd expected, but since I'd asked the Lord to prove to me He wanted me in the Army, He did!

"Before I leave the school." I prayed.

I had received a phone call at the front office and wondered what it could be this time! We were in the middle of practice for the graduation ceremony to follow tomorrow.

I already had my plane ticket for my return to Iowa.

"It's Brother Gannon, Les." He began, "I just received a call from the chief of chaplain's office. They've told me that they're going to take you on active duty, PRONTO."

I dropped the phone in excitement and shouted, "Praise the Lord!" This is it! This is it! The Lord had answered the fleece, completely!

I could hardly speak as I was so overcome with emotions. "They'll be in contact with you in a few days about your assignment." Dr. Gannon concluded after regaining my attention.

And yes, I was ready to go! Ready to go back into the Army.

No Man Can Close the Door Unless God Permits

"How many years you got in?" Chaplain J.D. Ford asked one day over lunch together. That opened the door for me to share with him now how the Lord brought me back into the Army. "I just came in, don't let this grey hair fool you." I said. They called me a green bean! This, in spite of my being older than most of the Chaplains at Ft. Polk.

And they hadn't even expected me. I wonder why?

"How long have you been in?" was the big question to really ask, "How long before you can retire." That is. Yes! That is what it is all about! Retirement! You can retire in 20 years if you can stand it that long.

Another would ask, "How long have you been in?" And soon I began to wonder about it, "Let's see, just how long have I been in?"

Not very long! Soon I added the years from back in 1956 when I'd been in the first time. Then I realized that if I'd stayed in when I was drafted, the very day I came back on active duty as a Chaplain, I could've retired, myself! Wow! That's incredible!

But God had only just begun with me! He had much in store for me. And Stan Miller, Deputy Chaplain, invited me over to his BBQ one night. "Tell me more about how you got in, Les." He said very curiously.

It seemed to me like the longer a person had been in the Army as a Chaplain, the further away from the Lord they were. I could see myself 20 years down the road, just another officer and not on fire for the Lord. Hanging on until retirement.

I told Stan about it and he absorbed it all. As he drove me home to my room at transient quarters that night, he confessed, "Les, I had you pegged as a Lutheran when I first saw you. I was surprised when I heard that you were here with the Assemblies!"

But all I did was go to my room. When I turned out the light on that night, I remember seeing the cockroaches run for cover. Hundreds of them; swarming all over my bed and everywhere. I have to sleep in here tonight? I thought.

Yes. Ft. Polk, Louisiana. I didn't see swamps or alligators until after about two years there. We were in the center of the Katachie National Forest.

And then there was the first Sunday I preached in good old Chapel #3 on South Fort. "I don't own a watch, so I don't know what time I'll finish this morning." I announced.

It wasn't long in coming after the service; I heard it, "I can see that we'll have to take up a collection and buy Chaplain Simonson a watch." One of the several Colonels that attended the chapel stated.

I recalled old uncle Carl, once again, "Good Sermon, but too long." I felt the rejection once again.

Services had to be run like everything else in the Army, on time with no surprises. I'd soon learn that. But I was flying high after seeing what the Lord had done to bring me in, so I didn't let it bother me.

Soon, Sharon and the kids joined me from Iowa. We had to stay in a little cottage on North Fort. A one-bedroom place, but the kids didn't mind a bit! They were so excited to see all of the military tanks and guns that it was an exciting time. Sharon had trouble adjusting though, doing the wash in the Laundromat or the barracks was a drag.

It was fun though as we all took it in stride. A whole new life for all of us; and lots of lessons to learn.

It felt exciting to be preaching again and it wasn't long before I found myself counseling the men from the unit during most of my time. Men with problems, all kinds of problems, like I'd never seen before. But it was exciting and I enjoyed it, every bit of it. But then the preaching seemed to be different. Sure, you had to be careful of what you said; yet wouldn't we be able to preach the word freely?

The guys that I counseled during the week needed to be in church on Sunday to hear the messages. They never showed up! It was only the General, Colonels and officers with families. In fact, I soon saw that it was kind of like the churches that I'd seen back home.

Sure, the people believed, but they didn't want to go too far with the Lord. Let's just keep it simple and safe. Don't go overboard.

"Who's going to be preaching this week?" an assistant asked as he took a phone call one morning. We had 3 Chaplains and took turns with preaching. The message was that some people preferred to hear certain preachers, and now we'd better get in line or else.

Guy Jolin, the senior chaplain suggested one day, "Why don't we have a preaching seminar-What do you say? We'll tape our sermons and then listen to them to learn from each other." I balked big time. "No way, man! I've been to the seminary and don't need a lesson on how to preach." I became defensive and resisted, feeling that the pressure was being put on to conform to the standards.

And it got worse as the days went on. Young chaplains have a lot to learn and that's where the older ones come in. Sure, I still had a lot of the old self in me and I could see that the Army was bringing it out once again. Some of the lessons I had not learned at the seminary or in Blairsburg would have to learned here.

And then there was Rich Minus. He came in as a green bean about six months after I got there. Rich was black and a Baptist. If that wasn't bad enough, he'd gone to Princeton. That made him famous. Then, I recalled what Leon Dickenson had said to me back in 1974, "If you were black or a female, I could help you out real quick!" I had not forgotten that and resented it more than a little.

But I'd give him a chance to prove himself, since I had to work with him in the chapel. He turned out to be quite a guy. I liked him a lot. He seemed to seek the same things of God that I did and we began to pray and seek the Lord together.

We prayed after work and sometimes during the noon hour at chapel #3. Prayer for revival among the chaplains, and for the church at Ft. Polk.

It wasn't long before the Lord touched Rick with the power of the Holy Spirit, just as He had touched me back in Iowa, three years earlier. It really fired him up and things began to happen.

"Chaplain Simonson, A.W.O.L."

This was the note that showed up on the door of the Division Chaplain on Monday morning. It all began the week before. We had a training accident. A man in my unit was killed. He was from Northern Minnesota. He left behind a Korean wife and 2 small children. The baby was only a couple of months old. It was a sad situation.

The young wife was hysterical, as we told her of the accident. She tried to commit suicide and refused to believe that it had happened.

Lots of people helped to try to prepare her to go to Minnesota with his body. They were going to put her on the plane alone and send her North. I just knew that she'd never make it, but the regulations didn't provide for any escort for her, only the body.

I told the commander, "Someone has got to go with her. I don't care what the regulations say!" He agreed and went to the General.

It all happened so quickly and finally I was elected to go. It was more than I had bargained for, however. It caused a lot of raised eyebrows among the other chaplains. They'd never seen anything like that done before.

I was looking out for the wife. She was grief struck and unable to cope with the situation. I was hopeful that once we got her to the husband's family, she would calm down.

The Army doctors said that she could travel, but would need support. We took off and barely made our flight from Ft. Polk, changing flights in New Orleans and transferred again in Chicago before flying to Duluth, Minnesota where we were met by the soldier's family.

It was a nightmare for me and for her. The baby was crying and was she. I prayed most of the way. That was all that I could do. The Lord helped us too! I knew that he was there beside us the entire way.

She'd been unable to see the body before we left, which made it worse. She still didn't believe he was dead. He'd been messed up pretty bad, too. I hadn't seen him either, so didn't know how he looked.

It was late the next day before we finally got the family together at the funeral home to view the body. That was unbelievable. It was a tragic situation. He was the only boy in a family of 5 sisters.

Finally, we opened the casket and saw him. She went into hysterical fits again, along with a couple of his sisters. We got the local doctor and he gave them a shot and sent them home. We made it through the day and finally the funeral.

What it showed me was that there is nothing as important as the need to have a funeral and time to view the body after a person dies. It's necessary to help work through the grief that goes along with death. Sure, I'd taken classes on death and dying in seminary. This was different now. I saw first hand how important it was and never forgot it.

And I had a new job when I returned. I wasn't sure if it was related to what had been going on before I left or because of my leaving in the way that I did. Of course, I had to learn that you didn't ask questions when the system decides to move you. You move and take it as the Lord is saying it's time to go on.

After all, hadn't the Lord put me in the Army in spite of the odds against it? Sure he had. So, I took it that the Lord was in charge and that I was to trust Him.

And there was the special night in chapel #3, just before I left. Rich and I were leading a worship service on Sunday night, together. We'd been praying late one afternoon for the service, "Help us to bring your Word to Your people in love." It was dark and quiet in the chapel. We were both at the altar. I saw a young man come in and sit down in the middle of the chapel. We continued to pray and praise the Lord. After several minutes I thought that I'd better go and see what our visitor required of us, perhaps he needed some counsel.

As I got up from my knees to do so, walking past Rich, I felt a strong leading to lay my hands upon Rich's head and to pray, "Lord, here is your servant. Please bless him and anoint him with your Holy Spirit. Make him wise and show him what you want for him to do while he is serving you here!"

All of the time that I was in prayer, I had a strange feeling that I needed to get to the young man sitting in the chapel. Finally, I did so. I turned to move back and talk to him, I saw him going toward the front entrance and walking out. I had a sinking feeling in my stomach and felt as if I had failed to answer to his needs. I felt I had let him down. Chaplains are supposed to help people!

Almost at a run, I headed for the door to try to catch him. It was only a few seconds as I got outside. I saw no one in sight. I ran around the back of the chapel and had circled to the front. By now, Rich had come outside. We were puzzled by this event. There was no possible way he could have escaped without our seeing him in that short of a time frame.

That left only one possibility. It had to have been an Angel. "Was it possible? Could it be?" We read the scripture in Hebrews, *"Be not forgetful to entertain strangers, for thereby some have entertained angels unawares."*[18]

"Forgive us Lord, we didn't mean it." We prayed afterward. We wondered if the Lord had sent the Angel to us to get together and pray for one another, since that was the first time we had done so. After that event, we prayed for each other much as the days flew by.

We were united, like David and Jonathan and as the days went by, we needed to have that support. Fire was about to fall!

"You offended that Chaplain when you spoke at that Chaplain's breakfast, Les." Rich told me. "The word was out around post that you talked for an hour about how bad the Lutheran church is!"

It mattered little that I hadn't said anything like that. That is the way that it came out.

It wasn't long after that they had moved Rich out of Chapel #3 too. He was getting too bold and it was time to go. The post Chaplain decided they needed a Black Gospel Service. Rich was against it. That mattered little. He'd have to go along with it.

It became the most popular service on the post in a few months. They

---

[18] The Book of Hebrews, Chapter 13, verse 2.

had moved me way up on North Fort. The Chaplain before me had been kicked out of the Army. He had been charged with sexual advances and a bunch of other stuff; a real mess.

I heard about it after I had been on the job a while. That helped little in trying to get started in the artillery unit.

They weren't too crazy about Chaplains after that situation. I continued to counsel and had plenty of business. All kinds of stuff; drugs and marriage problems; everyone trying to get out of some mess. Not interested in really going all the way with the Lord.

I talked to everybody I could about the Lord and the word soon got out. "This Chaplain, all he talks about is God. I went to see him for help with my marriage, and he preached to me."

It was hard on the ego to hear these reports, but I did thank God for the opportunity to witness.

Since he opened the door, I knew that no man could close it unless He permitted it!

There was time to do some fishing too. I even bought a nice big bass rig, fully equipped with depth finder and all. I would go out to Toledo Bend once in a while. It was neat and we even camped out there with the family several times. The boys water-skied and fished.

Yes, the Lord had opened the door all right! I'd been in a year and soon I'd have to decide if I should stay in or get out.

When I came in, it was for a three-year period. That gives the Army time to look at you and evaluate your progress. It also gives a person time to decide himself. I knew that the Lord wanted me in. I didn't know how long. I hoped it wouldn't be too long. I was still fighting the Lord and He knew it!

And I began to see more and more that the longer one stayed in the less of a chaplain he was and more the officer that he was. I had made the comment of Chaplain Gibbs one day in a staff meeting. He wasn't too excited about it either! I could tell.

Then, it happened! We had a large accident and three of our soldiers were killed in a car wreck.

They have a saying in the Army, "You only have to go to church one time in the Army! That's when you die."

Regulation and tradition says that whenever a soldier is killed, no matter how it happens, a Memorial service is held for the man. We had two Memorial services back to back for the 3 men. As it turned out, I got to preach for one of them. I'd been with the widow of the man almost all weekend. In fact, I'd been the one to tell her of the death.

"We are not to be the notifying office in the event of death." I told the Duty Officer that night after I called. "It doesn't matter, Chaplain, you're an officer and we need an officer. Time is running out and you've got to tell her." I was green and besides he was right. Someone has got to tell he before she finds out through other means.

Thankfully, she was a Christian herself. She had a young baby, too. The man had been a Christian for some time himself. He was an excellent soldier and respected in his unit. I knew that the service would be tough since the Colonel had invited the widow to the service.

She asked me to speak about her husband's faith and to tell the men. I knew this would be bad since these memorial services should be brief and without meaning, only to memorialize the soldier.

And I preached a powerful message. I never felt the anointing of the Holy Spirit more as I preached to a chapel full of soldiers who had been marched in.

The General was there. That was traditional too. He was hopping mad after the service. I could tell. Nothing was said until 2 days passed.

I received a call late at night form a senior chaplain, "You need to go and talk to Chaplain Gibbs, first thing tomorrow morning, Les." W.T. Permenter said. "It's about the memorial service. The General was mad and it doesn't look good. Good Luck!" he said.

I was anxious as I went to see Chaplain Gibbs. I didn't want to make trouble for the Chaplains Corps and it looked like I had.

"I'm afraid you're not going to make it in the Army as a Chaplain, Les." Chaplain Gibbs said. "Everybody knows, Les Simonson loves the Lord and all that, but when it comes to being a soldier and an officer, you can't cut it!" he continued. "This is just one example! I have many reports of the past couple years now that you are not interested in staff meetings, you'd rather read your bible or pray. The words even out around post that Les Simonson is a faith healer!"

He really laid it on me. Things came out that I had suspected, but never known for sure. At least, it was in the open now. That wasn't all! "I'm not alone in this, every senior chaplain on post feels the same way that I do. You'll never make it in the chaplaincy! I hope you understand. Nothing personal, Leslie. I like you, myself."

The bomb had dropped. I felt as though I had been run over by a truck. Nothing left in me.

There's more? I thought as Chaplain Gibbs continued, "I'd advise you not to apply for extended active duty. I will not approve it. I want you to know that it is within my power to decide if you should stay in or not. It's all up to me." He concluded.

I had to say something; I waited for the words to finally come out! " I respect what you're saying and I understand that you have to do what you think is right." I told him. "I think you understand how the Lord brought me on active duty I really didn't want to come, but when I say how he worked to bring me in, I know that He opened the door." Then I dropped the bomb on him. "It'll be up to the Lord if He wants me to stay in, not you! I hope you understand."

I recalled the words of the message that cold January night back in Iowa, "No man can open the door unless God permits."

I felt my gut tighten as I got up and dressed. I surely didn't want to make that call. "How did I ever get into this business? Why couldn't I have been a forest ranger, Lord?"

I knew better by now, but I had to get it out. Somehow I felt better when I did. I prayed in the Spirit for strength and guidance. It worked. It really worked.

"Just trust me and I'll take care of this situation too." The Lord seemed to assure me.

I reported at the scene and spoke with the MP in charge. "We got to try to stall him as long as we can! We need to stall him long enough to get in there and get the gun from him! If we can make him think that you're not here, it'll give us some time to think of something." He got no argument from me, I assure you.

I had no desire to go in with the man with the gun. I began to do a lot of praying. I mean, really praying! Not just words.

It worked. Before too long we worked it so that a couple of the guys got in close enough to get near and grab his gun. Thanks Lord, for that!

But that wasn't the end of it. I received a call the next morning. "Chaplain Gibbs needs to see you, Les." W.T. informed me. "What about this time?" I thought. I'd made it pretty rough for him the past several months.

"Did you call last night about a man in the hospital requesting to see a chaplain?" Gibbs stated. "This doesn't sound like something you'd do, Les, but the report is that the chaplain was called and he never showed up!"

I assured him that I was indeed there. He accepted it and was relieved. Of course, part of our plan had been to act like I hadn't gotten there, so at least that was effective.

I was pleased that Chaplain Gibbs was confident that I would have showed up. He was good man and I liked him. It's a tough job being a post Chaplain.

I felt I should go ahead and submit my paperwork for the indefinite status. Despite, if not because of what Chaplain Gibbs had professed earlier.

I put it in and it came back. Done wrong, was the verdict. "What does that mean Lord? Do I continue or drop it?" no answer came.

I knew that I had to trust the Lord to open the door or to close it. It happened late one night in December 1978. The telephone rang and it was W.T. on the other end, "Just had a call from Chaplain Gibbs. He says you should go ahead to submit the paperwork for extended active duty, if you want to. He's going to approve it."

Praise the Lord! No man can close the door unless God permit! That's exactly the way it happened.

"Oh, by the way, I almost forgot," W.T., added, "he also said to tell you to get your bags packed. You're headed for Germany in July!"

"No! No! Lord, no! Not Germany again." I muttered as I hung up.

The End of the Line

One morning after running with Colonel Widden, our 3-mile tradition was complete and we were in the Divarty Gym locker room showers before returning to daily work. "So, you're headed to Germany, are ya, Les."

He continued on without really looking for a response, " I wouldn't go back there again for anything. I'd go to Washington first. In fact, I'd cut my wrists first." I didn't know if he was serious or joking. Whatever the case, it didn't sound too good to me either.

Colonel Widden talked about the serious drug and family problems. I knew that he had problems there, but when he said that I wondered what would happen. I had lots of respect for the Colonel and knew that he was pulling my leg a little, but yet what he had said scared me.

That was only the beginning! There would be more before it was over. The days began to fly by. We had to get ready to leave Ft. Polk now and head for Germany. Lots of things to do and not much time to do them.

It was hard to imagine that we'd already been in the Army for 3 years. Time had gone by fast. What was that question? "How many years have you been in?" Oh, yes.

If I had stayed in from my first tour in I would have retired three years ago. Yes, I'd think about that many times. It was humbling. I needed it. It was also an opportunity to witness to tell others how the Lord is still working today and that miracles never cease. I knew that the Lord had worked it out that way.

All the things along the way had been for a purpose and now it was time to go to yet another place. But before we left Fort Polk, LTC Chapman, another one of my commanders, called me in his office. "I hear you got orders to Germany. Is it right that you are going to Camp Eschborn and the 317th Engineer Battalion? Chaplain, we really need you here, and we're going to miss you. But they need you worse over at Camp Eschborn!" he stated with a chuckle.

That sick feeling returned to my gut, "Why not someone else, Lord?" was my plea with the Lord for weeks after. I still hadn't come to terms with the Lord on this issue of being in the Army. I hadn't yet come to the end of the line. I knew it and the Lord knew it.

It reminded me of what Paul, the Apostle, had said to the church at Corinth,

"Sometimes I think that God has put us apostles as the very end of the line, like prisoners soon to be killed, put on display at the end of the victor's parade, to be stared at my men and angels alike."[34]

"I don't like to be stared at, Lord!" I guess that nobody does. Maybe that's why it's so hard for any of us to come to Him. We know deep down that that's what is going to be.

There had been times at Fort Polk when it looked like the end of the line. The end of the line as far as the Army was concerned.

We would be departing soon, we remembered some of the exciting times there in the South. Some of that excitement a symptom of the Deep South itself.

"Hello Chaplain Simonson, This is Reverend Jackson, Principal at the Christian School, just north of Leesville. Could you come out and speak to the students in the chapel service?" he asked by telephone. "I'd be delighted to do it!" was my quick response.

---

[19] I Corinthians 4:9

After all, I'd spent years in the schools and I enjoyed kids. It would be a great chance to share Jesus too.

When I arrived, the faculty and students warmly greeted me. After I finished speaking, I began to give out little crosses I'd brought along to the students.

Suddenly, Reverend Jackson blurted out, "Oh no, you can't do that! You can't give out those crosses! We don't believe in jewelry. You can't do that!"

I was shocked by his reaction, never giving it a thought that any group would be opposed to crosses. Then took out some wallet calendars with a picture of Jesus on them and started to distribute them to the kids. I thought for sure there would be no objection to that. I knew that the kids would like to have a little something to remember the visit.

Again, Reverend Jackson yelled out, "No! No! Chaplain, Not pictures! Jesus didn't have long hair and we don't believe in that! You can't pass out those pictures!"

And so it was that I learned how narrow and secretarian we can become. I'd seen this before coming to Louisiana, but now it seemed as though it might be worse here that up north.

Like the day the Sergeant came to see me. He was a member of my Battalion. "Chaplain, you've got to help me. I don't know what to do." He said, "I'm in big trouble with my company. I've been in the Army for 6 years and have had a real bad drinking problem. Just recently I went to a revival meeting with my neighbor. It was great! I gave my life to the Lord and haven't had a drink in 3 months," he told me, "But now, my pastor is telling me that I must not roll up the sleeves on my uniform. He says it's not in the Bible and it's wrong for me to roll them up. My unit's gonna give me a court martial if I refuse to do it! They say its Army regulation! What am I gonna do Chaplain!"

I didn't really know what to tell him. I felt angry with any pastor who'd tell a man such a thing and knew that was wrong. But, I told him to go and study the Bible for himself to find out what he should do. I wanted to tell him to forget about what his pastor had told him. I just couldn't do that. I was mad, I knew that, but not sure exactly at whom.

Sectretarian Denominationalism is a very sinister force. It's loose in the world today and we're all in danger of being caught by it. Yes, I'd been trapped in it for a long time, I knew that now. I guess that's why I had such strong feelings against it when I saw it.

Sometimes it seems like we, in the church, practice very little if any of what we preach. Like the time that past summer, just before the Bi-Centennial Celebration. A pastor form Vicksburg, Mississippi, called and asked me to speak at a special July 4th service he wanted to have for his community. But a few days before the date of the service, he called again, "Sorry to be calling you Chaplain, but I've got some trouble with the service here. This has not been done before and having a service in the Park, open to all, upsets members of my church. Some are afraid." He continued, much to my amazement, "That if we have it, some of the Indians and Blacks that live around here might come to the service!"

I could hardly believe my ears! Could this be happening? I thought sure those days were gone. I learned that day that many so-called Christian churches, though they preach against racism and discrimination, practice it freely. I didn't want to believe it. "I'm totally against it," said the pastor. At least I was glad to hear that. "I've already resigned as pastor here and will be moving back to Texas next month," he told me.

Sure, I'd heard and read about the trouble President Carter had with his home church back in Plains, Georgia. I thought what was an isolated case, now I wasn't so sure anymore. Especially not sure after 2 of my best Chaplain friends, Leon Bell and Bill Ackridge, returned to Ft. Polk from their denominational conference. And they were both members of the American Baptist Convention. But what they told me, shocked me, "It was Sunday morning, as we were driving through Mississippi. We decided to stop and attend church since we had time. We parked and headed for the church. As we were about to enter, we were met at the door by a couple of men. "You can't come in this church, we don't allow blacks in here!" (Leon Bell is very black and Bill Ackridge is very white!)

"We didn't go to church that day, but I did write a letter to the pastor of the church when we returned back here." Bill told me.

I was saddened and outraged at the same time. It's not right, but it's happening. Happening all over this country. All over the world. "Lord forgives us all! Lord helps us all!" If we don't do something about it soon the Lord may. It may be the end of the line for all of us, if we don't shape up.

Yes, we've been serving God on our terms for a long time now. I feel that the time is coming and sooner than we realize, when we're going to have to start serving God on His terms. The signs all point that way now! I'd been serving the Lord on my terms for a long time, and I guess He'd been accepting it But now that I'd been trying to serve Him on His terms these past few years, it seemed like I'd been getting into more and more hot water. And becoming more and more unacceptable.

That was it! I had to trust the Lord to see what he wanted. He'd have the final word. I knew that.

It bothered me to talk to Chaplain Gibbs like that, but I had to let him know where I stood. He seemed to understand, but I also knew he meant it!

And after that, W.T. Permenter, a good brother and Chaplain, told me "Les, the chaplaincy needs you more than you need the chaplaincy!" I didn't get what he meant. He tried to explain, but it was some time before I got it.

He was trying to tell me in a nice way to get out. He had been in a long time now and had been through a lot of frustration himself.

I knew he meant well, but couldn't help but think he'd been set up to encourage me to get out by Chaplain Gibbs. I had to seek the Lord on that one plus a lot of other things those days.

And then, as if this wasn't enough, right in the middle of all this, while on call as post duty chaplain, I got a call. It was 3a.m. "Chaplain, this is the MP desk. I've got a job for you. We have a man at the emergency room over at the hospital. He says he's going to blow his brains out! He wants to talk to a Chaplain before he does it! Can you come over right away!"

Can I come over right away! "Sure, I'll be right over." What else could I say? Maybe something like what I was really feeling; no way man! Call his unit Chaplain. Sorry I can't make it...

And the more I thought about that, the more I realized that it was with the church that I had most of my trouble, not the World. So, I wondered about that a lot, as I saw this entire act going on around me in Louisiana.

Of course, it didn't take me long to realize that Jesus had the same problem. But now as I got closer and closer to leaving, I wondered if the Lord really wanted me to go to Germany after all.

At least in Louisiana, I knew what I was up against. Not so in Germany. And from the report I'd gotten, it didn't look like something I wanted to get into.

I guess maybe, I felt a little of what old Paul must of felt as he was headed for Jerusalem. He had stopped over in Miletus on his way. And before leaving, called all the elder together down there by the boat and laid it on them, "*...and now I am going to Jerusalem, drawn there irresistibly by the Holy Spirit. He has told me in city after city that jail and suffering lie ahead...*"[20]

Not a very exciting message to leave the boys with, was it? But that's what it was and that's what it is today for us apostles. And I knew it, and I didn't like it. But I knew that it was better than doing it my old way. The way that I'd always done it before.

So, I was encouraged when I went on a little further in reading what Paul continued to say, "*...but life is worth nothing unless I use it for doing the work assigned me by the Lord Jesus- the work of telling others the Good News about God's mighty kindness and love...*"[21]

And so, I made preparations to leave Ft. Polk behind. But since we'd been unable to get concurrent travel, I'd have to leave Sharon and the kids behind. I decided to move them back to Wisconsin. They could stay with relatives. Not what we wanted, but everybody else had to do it, why not us?

And that's what we did! We moved them all in with Sharon's folks. Hoping it wouldn't be long before they'd be able to join me.

Saying goodbye to Sharon and the kids was the hardest we'd had in all of our years together. "I'll write every day and I'll call as soon as I get

---

[20] The Book of Acts, Chapter 20, verse 22, The Living Bible.

[21] Ibid, verse 20-22,23, The Living Bible.

there," I told Sharon very early Sunday morning, before I left.

It was July 15th 1979 and I had to be in Charleston, South Carolina, the next day. "We'll be praying for you every day, Les!" Sharon said before I left. I felt like I'd be needing it.

And as I started the Buick and headed out toward Madison, the 900 miles to Charleston seemed a long way off.

But I was thankful, at least, for the Buick. The Lord had made it possible for us to get it by working a real miracle. I'd never been able to afford anything but Fords, and now the Lord had given us this Buick. "We'll let you have it for $7,600.00 and not a penny less," the salesman said. Sharon and I had gone home and prayed about it. "That's a good price. It's only one-year-old, 12,000 miles. Besides, " I told Sharon, "it sold for just under $12,000.00 new."

But as we prayed, it seemed like the Lord was saying, "Offer them $6,700.00." I called them and made the offer. "No way, Chaplain. That's way under our wholesale cost," he told me. "Just a minute, the boss just came in, let me talk to him." I waited for a few minutes until his voice returned to the line; "You've got the money today, and have you Chaplain? If so, it's yours if you want it." And sure enough, we had a new Buick. We needed a big car and it worked out just fine for our family.

But now, as I set out, it seemed empty without Sharon and the kids. I wasn't used to having it so quiet driving. No fighting kids and no one to talk to.

The first 300 mile were the worst, as I drove south, past Madison and on by Chicago, alone. We wanted to take it with us. Sure it took more gas than smaller cars, but we needed the room and couldn't bear the thought of leaving it behind.

And I had lots of time to think and talk to the Lord on that trip. "Lord, I really don't want to go! I guess you know that, right?" I told Him. Of course that wasn't anything new to Him. It had been the story of my life, running away from the Lord and not wanting to do what He wanted me to do.

Hopefully, I had learned a thing or two by now. I sometimes wondered.

It had looked like the end of the line many times in recent years and somehow; the Lord had opened the door. It had caused me lots of embarrassment. And I kept thinking of Paul. "*...And now I'm going to Jerusalem, drawn there irresistibly by the Holy Spirit, not knowing what awaits me, except that the Holy Spirit has told me in city after city that jail and suffering lie ahead...*"[22]

But how I tried, for so long, to avoid this. Not wanting to suffer, I'd gone the way of the world for so long. And I guess that was why I'd tried so hard to be accepted and make it big in the world. So I'd be popular. Always telling myself along the way that then I'd be of greater use to the Lord. I'd have more influence for Him Yes, being accepted had always been important to me. Rejection always hurt me.

But somehow, now I was learning that I need that if I was to be useful to the Lord. Hadn't Fort Polk been an example of that? After all, Paul had something to say on that subject, "*...Notice among yourselves, dear brothers, that few of you who follow Christ have big names or power or wealth. Instead, God has deliberately chosen to use ideas the world considers foolish and of little worth in order to shame those people considered by the world as wise and great....He showed us God's plan of salvation; he was the one who made us acceptable to God...*"[23]

Sure enough, Christ had made us acceptable to God. The more acceptable we came to Him, the more unacceptable we became to the world. The Lord seemed to say to me, "Yes, when you're upside-down, you're right-side up!" Upside-down in the world's eyes is right side up in God's eyes. That makes sense.

But still, it wasn't easy. "Nobody ever said that it was going to be, did they?" All the stuff along the way. Getting thrown out of the seminary, the persecution afterwards, all the embarrassment that went along with getting in the Chaplaincy, and then almost getting kicked out. But then I remembered what Paul had said somewhere, "*Sometimes I think God has put us apostles at the very end of the line, like prisoners soon to be killed, put on display at the end of a victor's parade, to be stared at by men and Angels alike...*"[24] It seemed to make sense, of course. Who likes to be on the "end

---

22 The Book of Acts, Chapter 20, verse 22-23, The Living Bible.

23 I Corinthians I, Chapter 1, verse 26-30, The Living Bible.

24 I Corinthians, Chapter 4, verse 9, The Living Bible.

of the line"?

Yes, it would have been easy to turn around and head back to Wisconsin. The end of the line, Charleston, and then go on to Germany didn't look too inviting then. I didn't want to go!

And looking at the gas gauge, I thought, "I guess I'd better stop and get some gas before I run out. It looks like I'm getting pretty good gas mileage, at least, I've come almost 300 miles." But as I pulled into the oasis, I thought to myself, "Why not just turn around and go back now! They don't need you over there in Germany. Besides, remember what hell you went through over there?"

And then I looked at the cross around my neck, and read, "THY WILL BE DONE". Okay, Lord, I get the message. I realized once again, that walking with Jesus meant doing many things I didn't want to do. What was it that preacher had said back at Ft. Polk, "Faith knows that the further we go with Jesus, the fewer options we have!"

That night when I stopped for the much-needed rest at a small motel in the hills of East Tennessee, I rested securely in the assurance that though I was alone, I wasn't really alone at all.

The Lord Himself was with me by His Spirit. He was also with Sharon and the kids, back in Wisconsin. I would give us all the strength to endure. Endure whatever it was ahead at the end of the line.

I'd leave early the next morning to drive on to Charleston to catch that Port Call that would take me on to Frankfurt, Germany and the new assignment.

I boarded the plane; with my Bible opened, I read it carefully;

"But life is worth nothing unless I use it for doing the work assigned me by the Lord Jesus- the work of telling others the Good News about God's mighty kindness and love..."[25]

As the plane lifted, I read the passage again and drifted off into a deep and restful sleep.

---

[25] The Book of Acts, Chapter 20, verse 24, The Living Bible.

A New Door

It was the last day of January 1980, as the large C5A taxied down the runway at Rein Main Air Force Base. "Fasten your seat belts and extinguish all smoking materials," the pilot announced. "We'll be departing in a few minutes. Welcome aboard flight number WF3Y, destination, Dover, Delaware. Flight time is approximately 9 hours." He concluded.

I set myself for the take off. As I did so, I thought at once about the message that I have received the previous evening.

The telephone rang around Midnight. "Good Evening, Chaplain, this is Lieutenant Wells, Battalion Staff Duty Officer. I have a Red Cross message for you," he said. "Another night out, to deliver the message," I thought as he continued. "This message is number WZ 34896574, received 29 January 1130 hours, message reads," he was a little hesitant as I awaited his news.

These Red Cross messages are a regular part of the Chaplain's duties. We are involved in them every day and many late hours of the night. So, I thought little of it until Lt. Wells read the message.

"Lyle G. Simonson expired on 28 January, at 2130 hours in Wild Rose, Wisconsin hospital. Funeral arrangements pending. Call brother

Boyd at once. That's all Chaplain. I'm sorry to have to give you this news," he said. "Is there anything that I can do for you?"

It was a very strange feeling, as I stood there, phone in hand being told that my father had died. I'd heard dozens of these messages before, but this was one that I wasn't ready for.

Dad had not been well for a long time, but he was now at home and it came as quite a shock.

I quickly called Boyd and talked further about the arrangements for Dad's funeral. Then, I'd gone into the bedroom, knelt by the bed and cried a prayer for Dad and asked the Lord to help me with the details, and to be with our Mother as she grieved.

It wasn't long before we had made all of the necessary arrangements and I was off to the airport. Sharon and the kids would stay home. It was too far to go, and besides with 3 teenagers in high school, they would miss more school than they could afford.

The Red Cross message came just a little over 6 months after I had arrived in Germany. A lot had happened during that time. I arrived in July with Sharon and the kids arriving in August, just before the start of the fall term. The boys, Tim and Phil had arrived just in time to start football, which was what they had been hoping they'd be able to do.

I'd received a pinpoint assignment to Eschborn. Words cannot describe how I felt when I first saw the place. "This is the smallest chapel in operation and the only Quonset hut chapel still in use," Chaplain, Col. Dick Tuppy, the V Corps Chaplain told the congregation that Sunday while introducing me.

There were around 16 soldiers and their families there to welcome me. All of them were excited to have a new Chaplain for themselves. But my excitement wasn't all that great, as I wondered what I had done to deserve this assignment, as the admonition of Colonel Chapman echoed in my thoughts, "We need you here, Chaplain, but they need you worse at Eschborn!"

In addition to that, there was the prophecy I'd received through Aquila Wilkens, just before leaving Ft. Polk. We'd been going to the Charismatic Teaching Center at Leesville, the hear her speak. Her ministry is well known and highly respected; that evening had been a true blessing as she gave us that powerful word.

We had gone expecting, Sharon and I, and that is when we would always receive from the Lord. Our hearts and spirits had been stirred as she spoke:

"I want to say a word to my brother, for a new door. Yes, I see a new door opening unto you. And as God does open the door, be ye faithful to walk therein. But it shall seem strange to thy natural mind, but thy spirit shall say, "ah, this is it, this is it!"

For God has caused thee to be drawn aside that He might season thee, that He might teach thee, that He might show thee a more perfect way. And now He would say, "Now is the time to come forth into the place in which I have called thee, for all that has taken place in the past, has been a time of teaching, a time of seasoning, for a more perfect day."

And the Lord would say, " the more perfect day has dawned upon thee. And thou shall go in great strength, and thou shall go in great power. And the anointing of God shall destroy the yoke from off of my people, because the anointing that shall rest upon these. Saith the Lord.""[26]

I thought for sure, the new door would mean leaving the Army Chaplaincy and moving back to Wisconsin. I just knew it! But that door never opened, and now here I was in Germany.

This had to be the new door, the Spirit talked about; it just had to be. It is so easy for us to get ahead of the Lord. We'd definitely done that.

Expecting the Lord to put us in the ministry back in Menomonee where we'd gone to graduate school several years earlier. We'd seen a ministry there to the university students and the community. We expected an Evangelistic ministry of some sort.

Now, here we were at Camp Eschborn. It had to mean this was the new door. At least I'd walked through it, and to be sure, it did seem strange to my natural mind.

We felt confident that the Lord wanted us here.

---

[26] Prophecy delivered by Aquila Watkins, Leesville, LA, 1979.

One of the first things we learned was that the Chaplain was not considered to be an indispensable part of the life of the Battalion. "The Chaplain who was here before you was treated just like a private," was the comment I heard one day from a well-meaning assistant. But I didn't let that stop me. After all, this was the new door the Lord had opened. He'd take care of the details.

It hadn't taken long to see that the morale was low. It was lower than I'd seen morale anywhere before. Trying to talk to the command about it, however, soon revealed to me that they didn't want to hear about it. "You can help us best here in the battalion, Chaplain, by being out among the soldiers, talking to them, on the job," was Colonel Muller's advice.

Soon I had the feeling that the Chaplain here would be viewed something like a Cuckoo clock. Coming out once in a while to do my thing, and then returning back in to be silent.

Or, perhaps, like one man said when asked how he viewed the Chaplain, "I see the Chaplain kind of like the Queen of England. Just a title with little or no influence or power!"

Then, I remembered the prophecy. I sought the Lord and He showed me He had everything under control. "Just trust me, I have opened this new door unto you, for a more perfect day!"

It didn't take long for me to see the needs; alcohol and drug abuse was high. Due, in part, to the long workdays and the frequent field duties.

"Where's my Jeep and tent?" I asked the XO, as we got ready to move out on our first field exercise. "You don't need a Jeep, Chaplain. You can hitch a ride where you need to go. Then, after a day or two, you can catch another ride to the next unit." He informed me.

This was something that I hadn't seen before. I felt like making a big stink about it, but the Lord seemed to say to me. "Trust me, for the more perfect day has dawned upon thee!" That is what I tried to do.

We were now airborne and on our way to Dover, Delaware. As we climbed to 30,000 feet, it began to get colder and I covered myself with a blanket issued just before we took off. Not exactly first class, but the price was right.

I couldn't sleep. The loud roar of the engines was deafening. I wondered why they'd given us earplugs, since they didn't seem to be of any help.

My mind wandered, as I lay motionless under the blanket. My thoughts were of Dad and all that he'd meant to me; of my family in Wisconsin; Sharon and the kids; the new door opened to my own life and finally, us. It had been a long road that had finally brought me to that day. "What will the future hold?" I wondered as I lay there.

Dad was 37 when I was born. I resented that along the way. Mainly when I saw other kids doing things with their Dads that mine never did with me. I remembered that Dad would have been 80 this October. He was born in 1900, which made it easy to calculate his age. He had never ridden on an airplane. I'd been half way around the world on a couple of occasions.

Yes, it's an incredibly exciting life, being an Army Chaplain. The travel is part of it, but somehow it never seems as exciting as they make it out to be in the recruiting posters and ads.

But Dad had lived an exciting life and had never left Mt. Morris. Hard work was something he was used to and seemed to enjoy it. I never remember him turning down a person who needed help.

I recall one hot, summer day. I was only 4 at the time. It has been told and retold through the family, although I don't remember, the excitement of that day.

"You stay in the truck, Leslie, I'll be right back," Dad said as he left me alone in the old Model A. We'd been on the routine ice route, delivering ice every winter and packed deep under dry sawdust. When summer came, Dad would sell the ice. I liked being with Dad and helping him with the ice route. I'm sure that I wasn't any help, but that didn't seem to matter.

It was a hot day and the truck was running hot, too. Now, Dad had stopped by our home to give himself and the old Model A a drink. Alone in the truck, I climbed up on the drivers seat, pretending to be driving myself. Getting a little carried away, I really became involved in my driving.

All at once, I lost my balance and slipped off the steering wheel and fell down on the seat. "Help! Help!" I yelled, as I hit the floor. The floorboards had been removed, I suppose for air circulation or because of previous repairs to the truck. As I fell, I hit the hot manifold pipe, landing on my right arm. "Daddy, Daddy, Bah! Help!" I screamed at the top of my lungs, as Dad came running around the corner of the house to see what had happened.

I'd been severely burned and they rushed me to the hospital where I would stay for several days. I still carry a big "4" scar on my right arm as a memento. I used to call it a potato chip in later years as I watched hair grow around the scar, but not on it. Dad never talked much about that day, but I knew that it hurt him deeply.

There was also the excitement of Bass fishing. Dad was the best in the county. During the war years and after, we had men coming to stay with us for a week or two at a time, just to fish for Bass. Dad would leave with them early in the morning and return late in the day.

The men came mostly from Chicago and Milwaukee. In those days that was a long trip and you had to stay for a while to make it worth the effort of the travels. They were all good, friendly men. And us boys waited expectantly for their return so we could help them bury the fish deep under the sawdust, on the ice. This would keep them frozen until they got ready to leave, when they'd pick them up and pack them in ice so they'd keep for the long trip back to the cities.

Yes, Dad had lots of work to do, during the summertime, but he'd manage somehow to get it done and still have time for fishing. He loved to fish Bass.

Now, all that I had left of Dad were the memories. I was grateful; at least that Dad had accepted the Lord just a few years earlier. "It's really important for you to make your peace with the Lord, Dad." I told him, while visiting in the hospital where he'd been taken after suffering his first heart attack. He'd never even been in a hospital before that day.

"I know I should, Son, but it's just so hard for me to do. I guess I'm just not good enough. I've done some pretty bad things in my life. Besides, I haven't gone to church much for many years," he told me. He was crying now as the tears ran down his cheeks, we prayed together that he'd ask the Lord to forgive him of all his sins and take him unto Himself.

It was an exciting day for me as I saw the Lord begin to work in Dad's life. He stuck with it and went through some pretty rough times, but never gave up and continued to trust the Lord. He had never been much of a churchgoer, but I always knew that he believed. I could tell by the way that he lived. I wanted to be just like him when I grew up.

But it was different, a lot different. I'd always been stubborn and determined. Dad was patient and easy-going. He was quiet and self-assured.

I remember that summer day in 1948. I was eleven and it had been a rough day. "I'm not going to do it, and that's final!" I screamed at my Mother. I was furious.

Dad had just come home. I usually watched myself when he was around, but it had slipped out. "Do what your Mother has told you, Leslie and do it now!" Dad ordered. I stomped out the back door and slammed the screen extra hard as I did. "I'm leaving! I'm running away from this place and never coming back!" I yelled as I headed down the road.

I knew that Dad was mad and I'd better clear out, I thought as I headed up the miller hill towards the cow pasture. "I'll be safe there. And besides, Dad can't catch me with his bad leg." I thought as I glanced over my shoulder. Sure enough, there was Dad, hot on my trail. I picked up my pace as I saw him coming.

"What am I going to do now?" I thought. "He's mad as a hornet and when he gets mad, things happen!" As I kept going, I'd look over my shoulder kind of pretending that I didn't know that he was coming.

I started to sweat as I crossed the old log gat into the pasture. "How long can I go on? Where is it going to end? What's going to happen to me when he catches me?" I was scared. I could see that Dad wasn't going to quit and that I had to do something. Finally, I did. "I'm going to stop and take my whipping, after all, I deserve it. I should have never been talking back to Mother in the first place."

I recall just sitting down on the hillside and waiting for Dad to catch up to me. I was shaking as the fear escalated with each step that he took. As he gained ground, a strange thing happened. As Dad approached, he didn't whip me at all. He spoke, " Come on son, and let's go home. We'll be late for supper now." As he took my hand and we headed back toward town, he even put his strong arm around my little shoulder as we walked together that day. It was one of the happiest moments of my life as I could just sense his love for me.

He had never been one to show much emotion by touch. We never did any hugging or kissing in my family. We just accepted that we were loved. This incident has communicated to me what a loving and concerned Dad I actually had.

I'd remembered then, and now, how as a very young lad I'd love to run into Mom and Dad's bedroom on an early Saturday morning and crawl into bed and have Dad put his big strong arm under my little head, and just lay there. I needed that and cherished every moment of it.

"I want to be just like my Dad when I grow up!" I thought as I lay there under the blanket on that freezing C5 aircraft at 40,000 feet above the earth.

I remembered how hard I had tried to please Dad along the way. How proud He'd been of Boyd and me when we both made the football team. How proud and pleased he seemed to be when I landed my first large Lunker Bass. How well He'd taken it when I announced that I was going to marry Sharon. As hard as it must've been for him, he never let it show. He had character.

I just knew he was so pleased when I finally announced that I'd decided to enter the seminary. He wasn't an emotional man, but yet he seemed to be filled with great emotion. He just didn't express it in ways that others did. I realized that and also realized that I'm just like my father in that respect. I've always been a feeling person. Maybe that is why I've been so sensitive to rejection, having trouble expressing my feelings by keeping them buried deep inside myself. But, I knew that I was on the right track. I just knew that I never wanted to return to my old ways. It wasn't worth it.

"Fasten your seatbelts, please! We are beginning our descent for arrival at Dover, Delaware. Please observe the no smoking signs and we hope that you've enjoyed your flight. You'll be happy to know folks, the temperature in Dover is 64 degrees," the pilot informed us. It had been 35 degrees upon leaving Frankfurt, 8 hours earlier.

I began to feel the huge craft sink slowly, ever so slowly and I couldn't help but think of those words of Paul from the book of Acts. Somehow they seemed to be spoken just for me; "*but life is worth nothing unless I use it for doing the work assigned me by the Lord Jesus- the work of telling others the Good News about God's mighty kindness and love.*"[27]

That is what life's all about. I thought about my own life and telling others about the Good News and God's mighty love and kindness. I realized that this is what the Lord had been telling me in the prophecy that I'd received back in Louisiana. The new door had opened and the more perfect day had dawned upon me.

> *"For God has caused thee to be drawn aside that He might season thee, that He might teach thee, that He might show thee a more perfect way. Now He would say, now it is time to come forth into that place into which He has called thee. For all that has taken place in the past, has been a time of teaching, a time of seasoning for a more perfect day..."*[28]

No, that place wasn't Camp Eschborn, nor was it Menomonee, or any other place. It was a place of resting and trusting in the Lord so that His anointing may rest upon me.

"*And thou shall go in great strength and thou shall go in great power. And the anointing of God shall destroy the yoke from off my people, because of the anointing that shall rest upon thee, saieth the Lord.*"[29]

Then I was reminded of the verses in Proverbs.

> *"We can make our plans, but the final outcome is in God's hands. We can always "prove" that we are right, but is the Lord convinced? When a man is trying to please God, God makes even his worst enemies to be at peace*

---

27 The Book of Acts, Chapter 20, verse 24.

28 Op cit.

29 Prophecy of Leland Davis, Dows, Iowa, February 1975.

> *with him. A little gained honestly, is better than a great wealth gotten by dishonest means. We should make plans counting on God to direct us..."*[30]

These passages seemed to sum up Dad's life so well. He had always tried to do right and, in his own way, always put the final outcome in God's hands. I knew of no enemies that Dad had. God had taken care of that, too.

What little Dad had, he had gained honestly. His honesty had been the trait that had impressed me the most during my high school years. As an insurance salesman, he stood tall, no matter what the test, in a profession that is known for its share of shady characters. As the saying goes, "We shoot every third salesman, the second one just left..."

But the part about making plans bothered me some. "I'd done so much of that, and where had it taken me?" I thought. He had me there. So content to just let things happen, just putting the final outcome in God's hands. I had been just the opposite, making big plans, forgetting about the Lord. On top of that, always "proving" that I was right, and yet knowing all along that the Lord wasn't convinced.

But it was different now. Everything was different now! Ever since that day at the altar of St. John's in Grinnell, Iowa.

"Come with me! See what I can do!" the Lord told me. I'd finally been able to let the Lord begin to direct me, still making the plans, but putting the final outcome in His hands.

Oh sure, there were problems. In fact, there were more problems than before. Then I knew that my life would be worth nothing unless I used it for doing the work assigned to me by the Lord Jesus- the work of telling others the Good News about God's mighty kindness and love!

It was then that I remembered Paul. "Can you come over here, right away, Chaplain! I've got a man here who says he's going to kill himself. He needs some help!" the First Sergeant of Bravo Company said late one night over the telephone. And sure enough, it was Paul. I'd seen him a couple of

---

[30] The Book of Proverbs, Chapter 16, verse 1-9, The Living Bible.

weeks back about sending his wife and child back to the United States early. "She's had an affair with another man, Chaplain, and I don't know what else to do." He had told me. He was drunk and in no shape to talk, but I could see that he was very depressed. "I just couldn't help it, Chaplain. We had another big fight. I got drunk and wanted to end it all. I just took the car and headed out, wanting to die! I was so angry. I just drove right into that German car and before I knew it, the police had me. Now I'm in big trouble. I'll probably lose my rank!"

We talked more that night and also into the next day after he'd slept off the affects of the alcohol. "I think I'm going crazy, Chaplain. I don't know what to do!" I tried to tell him of the Good News of God's mighty kindness and love, but I could see this was of no interest to him. "I need to talk to a psychiatrist, Chaplain!" I agreed to his request and had an emergency appointment issued to him.

A few days later, I received another call. "Paul's in the hospital," his wife told me. "He took an overdose of the pills the doctor gave him and he tried to jump from the third floor balcony at home. You've got to help him, Chaplain! I'm afraid he's going to kill himself and maybe me too!" was her desperate plea.

When I met Paul again, he seemed even more despondent than before. We talked at great length and once again, I felt the strong leading to tell him about the Lord and how He could help him through his problems.

As I did so, he seemed interested in what I had to say. I told him how he'd have to quit trying to handle his life by himself and trust the Lord to do it for him. "It's the only way I know of that works, Paul," I said, "I'm willing to try Chaplain. Nothing else has worked, that's for sure." He said as we kneeled down together in my office.

"Lord, please come and help my friend, Paul. He needs your help and you are the only one that can help him now. Forgive him for all of his sins. Take control of his life and make him the kind of person you want him to be. And if he's not sure he wants you to, do it anyway Lord," I prayed, since I wasn't exactly sure if he did or not. I could feel the presence of the Lord as we prayed together. Somehow, he seemed much calmer now that we had finished praying. It was like he knew that everything was going to be okay.

Yes, Paul still had problems, but as the days passed, I could see that Paul was changing. "Will you come with me and be there when I get my Article 15 before the Battalion Command, Chaplain?" he asked one day. "I don't expect you to say anything or help me to get anything less than I have coming. I'd just like you to be there." I went with him and heard him tell the Commander how he had turned to the Lord, and how He was helping him now.

As the huge C5A Galaxy hit the runway at Dover AFB, I knew I would soon be back in Mt. Morris where it had all begun. Just in time for my father's funeral, which would bring more opportunity to tell others the Good News about God's kindness and love. I could hardly wait to get there.

Soon after the funeral was over, I'd find myself back in Germany, at Camp Eschborn. During my time there, I would see many more "Pauls". Each time that I did, I'd tell them about Jesus and His wonderful love. Some listened and some didn't. The names were different, but the story was always the same.

It was at Camp Eschborn that I realized, I guess for the first time in my life, that the Bible means when it says, *"And we know that all that happens to us is working for our good and if we love God and are fitting into His plans..."*[31]

I could finally see that everything, yes, everything along the way had not been without a purpose. It was easy for me to relate to all the Pauls at Eschborn, or wherever I'd meet them as I continued to use the rest of my life to "do the work assigned to me by the Lord Jesus- the work of telling others of the Good News about God's mighty kindness and love."

Even the words of the prophecy from the Lord, given through His servant, Aquila Wilkins, back at Fort Polk, that I'd wondered most about, now took on meaning for me,

> *For God has caused thee to be drawn aside that He might season thee, that He might teach Thee, that He might show thee a more perfect way. And now He would*

[31] The Book of Romans, Chapter 8, verse 28, The Living Bible.

> *not say, not it is time to come forth into that place into which He has called thee. For all that has taken place in the past, has been a time of teaching, a time of seasoning, for a more perfect day..."*[32]

Now, I too, saw the new door the Lord had opened unto me. "Lord, help me to be faithful and to walk therein!"

[32] The Personal Prophecy of Aquila Wilkins, Leesville, Louisiana 1979.

Epilogue

Life goes on. With Eschborn behind us we moved on in the certainty that "all things would work together for good!" As the days, months, years roll on we continue to see how true this is. That does not mean that its always pleasant or what we would have , but the Lord is still the Lord and so we press on.. We press on with the memories, memories of how powerful the Lord is and how much we need Him.. We press on with the knowledge that life is not always fair. And with the knowledge and assurance that even though we can not see all of His plan, and how indeed it is working together for our good, He is still there, at work. I could not put it any better than Oswald Chambers, author of His Utmost for My Highest has put it, In speaking of our identification with Christ in our daily lives:

God does the arranging of our program. At certain stages of spiritual experience we feel we could do a lot if we could arrange the scene of our own martyrdom, but the Spirit of God reminds us that we do not choose the place of our offering. God has the setting of the saints life. Everyone who is born from above wants to be a missionary, It is the very nature of the Spirit they receive, viz., the Spirit of Jesus, and the Spirit of Jesus expressed in John 3:16;.....God keeps open house for the universe. We prefers to build up converts to our own point of view.........Are we prepared to be the disciples of our Lord Jesus in whom the glory of God is manifested? Can God see the manifestation of His Son's life in us? (*Complete Works of Oswald Chambers*, page 497)

Chambers goes on further and says that too often we are "speckled birds'. Meaning that not wanting to stand out as abnormal, odd , or eccentric, we go along with the crowd' when put in a corner, (as he would call it), and rather than confess Christ we deny Him. Chambers says what we should do is say; "No, I cannot take part in what you are doing because it would imperil my relationship to Jesus Christ." (Ibid. page 479) How true, and how many times I have done, and still do just that!

This is where the baptism of the Holy Spirit come into the picture.... "But ye shall be my witnesses..... and ye shall be Baptized with the Holy Spirit!..." Listen to what Chambers has to say on this point;

Why do we want to be baptized with the Holy Spirit? All depends on that "why" If we want to be baptized with the Holy Spirit that we may be of use, it is all up; or because we want peace and joy and deliverance from sin, it is all up. "He shall baptize you with the Holy Spirit," not for anything for ourselves at all, but that we may be witnesses unto Him.

To be consciously desirous of anything but that one thing is to be off the main track...As long as there is self -interest and self-seeking, something has to go (Ibid.p.479)

I wish I could say I was there, but all I can say, at this point, is that I am still trying and as the saying goes, "The Lord is not finished with me yet", I am a work in progress. That's what makes this life of "Following Jesus" so exciting .. Always something new. !

Like after we left Germany and returned to the states for attendance at the United States Army Chaplains School, Advanced Class at Fort Monmuth New Jersey. It was there that we learned that after graduation I would be assigned to Fort McCoy, Wisconsin... Where my military career had begun many years earlier with the Wisconsin National Guard... It was there that I would soon learn of my non- selection for promotion to

Major which meant that I would be leaving active duty for return to civilian life. (A story in itself that will be for another day or book.),, Little did I know that the Lord had more for me to do and as in the past, my life verse, Proverbs: 16;9, nailed it, "In his heart a man plans his course, but the Lord determines his steps." NIV.

I was planning to return to teaching or counseling or maybe pastor a small church somewhere but as it turned out He had some work for me once again where I had not planned or considered. The ministry with disabled veterans in the Department of Veterans Affairs Medical Center. It would be where we would see our three of our children graduate from college, marry and give some beautiful grandchildren. And face some more exciting challenges.

Then in 1998 we retired from the Veteran's Administration Chaplaincy and returned to Mt. Morris where I grew up...Where we now live in our live quietly in our log cabin in the woods.

It will take another book to fill in the details of these years but we will leave that for another time.

And so it was that the Lord directs our Steps and our Stops along the way... and so it is that lives are again touched. As we try to be faithful wherein he has placed us. Our purpose continues to be to Witness to the Lord and glorify Him. Always having to be careful not to let the pursuit of our goals. no matter how important they may seem to me, to cause me to lose sight of that purpose;

And we can that we can still say, as we did when leaving Camp Eschborn that Romans 8;:28, "And we know that all that happens to us is working for our good if we love God and are fitting into His plans." As we continue to use the rest of our days to "do the work assigned me by the Lord Jesus— the work of telling others the Good New about God's mighty kindness and love." Acts 20: 24. Living Bible.

"Lord help me to be faithful to walk therein!"